87 BOAT DESIGNS

87 BOAT DESIGNS

A Catalog of Small Boat Plans from Mystic Seaport

Benjamin A. G. Fuller

Mystic Seaport
Mystic, CT
2002

Mystic Seaport
75 Greenmanville Avenue, P.O. Box 6000
Mystic, CT 06355-0990

Mystic Seaport Museum.
    87 boat designs : a catalog of small boat plans from Mystic Seaport / Benjamin A. G.
Fuller. — Mystic, Conn. : Mystic Seaport, 2002.
    p. : ill., plans ; cm.

    1. Mystic Seaport Museum - Catalogs. 2. Naval architecture - Designs and plans -
Catalogs. I. Fuller, Benjamin A. G. , 1945- II. Title. III. Title: Eighty-seven boat
designs.

VM361.M9 2002
ISBN 0-913372-97-8

To Ellen C. Stone, Helen Packer,
and the Ships Plans Collection crew, past and present

CONTENTS

DOUBLE-ENDED PULLING BOATS

SCULL FLOATS AND DUCK BOATS

CAT-RIGGED BOATS

YAWLS AND KETCHES

POWERBOATS

OARS AND SAIL PLANS

MYSTIC SEAPORT PLANS LIST AND ORDERING INFORMATION

Introduction

From the mid-1970s to the late 1980s, visitors climbing the stairs to the Curatorial Department at Mystic Seaport were greeted by a blueprint machine in a corner. Then they met Helen Packer, who was in charge of the machine. She handled boatbuilding classes and boat shop inquiries, made copies of Mystic Seaport vessel and boat plans, and filled orders for plans. Most of these visitors were sent over to us by Eleanor Watson, chief interpreter in the Museum's boat shop exhibit. Others contacted us after reading articles by the Museum's associate curator for small craft studies, John Gardner, published in the *National Fisherman*.

The actual "catalog" of the plans collection was a simple printed list of boats, arranged by propulsion, rig, and size, much like the current list of boats included at the end of this book. A few of the plans were published to accompany the photos and brief descriptions of the Museum's entire watercraft collection in Maynard Bray's *Mystic Seaport Museum Watercraft* (1979). But there was no way for a prospective purchaser to evaluate plans without visiting the Museum.

For this catalog, I selected mostly smaller and lighter boats under 20 feet: boats that I and others interested in traditional small craft might wish to own or use; ones that (with a few exceptions) could live on a trailer in a garage when out of the water. Almost all of the boats are part of Collection 7, which is one of more than one hundred collections, or about 100,000 plan sheets, in the Mystic Seaport Ships Plans Collection.

A few of the plans included here are in the Miscellaneous category, which includes boats in other museum collections, or owned by individuals, who have permitted the lines to be taken off and plans drawn up, something much appreciated. Boats in the collections of the Adirondack Museum, the Antique Boat Museum, and the Independence Seaport Museum are included in this catalog and can also be obtained directly from those museums.

Most of the plans in Collection 7 were drawn of accessioned boats in the Museum's collection, or of boats built as part of the Museum's small craft program. These plans were drawn up as part of research projects, not as part of freshly crafted, fully tested naval architectural projects. This means, for example, that all plans need to be lofted, and not every construction detail is as completely delineated as a builder might want. Nevertheless, many amateur builders have successfully modeled or built these boats. But when you order plans you will find them stamped: "For Research Only. This plan is not certified for construction purposes. This copy is reproduced from the historic collection of the Ships Plans Division and may not be reproduced, published, or distributed in any form without the written permission of Mystic Seaport Museum, Inc. The Museum makes no warranty as to the accuracy of these plans or their usefulness for any specific purpose." Nor does the Museum warrant the safety of these designs. Anyone choosing to build these boats does so at their own risk and has sole responsibility for the use made of the plans and any liability therefrom.

With that in mind, these are designs that are well suited to the needs of builders, modelers, and researchers of traditional small craft, boat designs that are well within the means and budget of the amateur. Plans drawn under the supervision of John Gardner were generally measured to the inside of the planking and lofted as part of the drawing process. John's typical process was to take sections using a template and a spiling block, then go to a lofting table for the first draft. Some plans are rich in construction details—at least details that could be determined without disassembling the boats. In this book, the plans are not published as drawn; elements have been selected to convey the shape and construction of each boat. The plans sheets have many more details, often including offsets (when marked with a O in the plans list).

Mystic Seaport began documenting its small craft in the 1960s, contracting with naval architect Edson Shock.

With the arrival of John Gardner to develop the Museum's small-boat program in 1969, it took off. The University of Michigan-trained naval architect Robert Pittaway was hired by John in 1973, and you will find that most of these plans are the result of Rob's work. His career, sadly, was cut short by illness in 1978. John's other boat shop assistants, Ned Costello, Alison Pyott, Val Danforth, Julia Rabinowitz, and notably Bill Mills continued to contribute plans, as did John. The crew of the exhibit boat shop, now the John Gardner Boat Shop, also contributed plans of boats they were building, and you will find plans here by Ed McClave, Clark Poston, Barry Thomas, and Chris Rawlings. A few boats were drawn on contracts with the late boat historian and builder Bob Baker and with Dave Dillion. In the 1990s the Museum turned to volunteers for most small boat documentation. The late Andy Steever gave Mystic Seaport a set of his St. Lawrence River skiff plans and the rights to use them, and Andy Chase sent along a set of his plans with the boat he donated. Peter Vermilya, associate curator for the small craft collection, has organized a volunteer documentation crew, and Robert Grover, Bill Welte, Robert Allingham, and Roger F. Hughes of that group have work represented here. Notably absent from this catalog are plans by Bob Allyn, the longtime naval architect in the Museum's Henry B. duPont Preservation Shipyard, whose considerable work is to be found in drawings of Mystic Seaport's larger or more elaborate craft, ranging from the whaleship *Charles W. Morgan* to the Herreshoff 12-1/2. These plans are part of the full list of Collection 7 in the back of this book and are of especial interest to modelers. Without the hundreds of hours of work by these skilled people, this collection and this catalog would not be possible. Nor would this catalog have been completed without the photographic work of Judy Beisler of the Museum's Photography Department and the design work of Irwin Bag and Linda Cusano.

This was a tough book to write. Having spent 12 years as curator at Mystic Seaport, I knew the collection pretty well. But as you look at the boats you want to start building, or modeling, or at least trying examples of them at Mystic Seaport's boat livery. I began to look forward to the Museum's annual June Small Craft Workshop in January. What a thing it would be to see all of these boats together, to step from one to another, comparing and contrasting, and to try them out under oar or sail. In writing, I tried to feel the swing under oars, to sense the boat heel under foot or sail, and to hear the water runnning past.

It was hard too, because of the people. John Gardner who led this effort is gone now these seven years. Rob Pittaway, his chief assistant, was forced by his health to retire. Other shop assistants have scattered and moved on. Barry Thomas and Willets Ansel, who built many of these boats, have retired, as has Dave Dillion, who drew a number of these plans as a free lancer. So have Helen Packer and Eleanor Watson, who so ably supported the Museum's small craft efforts. Although quite a bit of the drawing had been accomplished before I arrived at Mystic Seaport in 1978, I do remember much of it, and several expeditions to gather data. Maynard Bray might call and tell us of some boats that needed measuring, or that we should pick up, or the call might come to Peter Vermilya, who is now the associate curator for the small craft collection. Leafing through the plans reminds me of the acrid smell of the blueprint machine outside the office door, with Helen Packer pulling plans for some visitors who had been sent up from the boat shop by Eleanor Watson, while I talked with them about which boat to pick.

The ships plans collection is now part of the Museum's G.W. Blunt White Library. After a string of temporary locations, under the leadership of Ellen C. Stone the collection moved into a magnificent home as part of the Museum's new Collections Research Center. When Ellen Stone published the *Guide to the Ships Plans Collection at Mystic Seaport Museum* in 1995, there were 111 cataloged collections, representing over 79,000 plans. More keep coming. Anne and Maynard Bray in their *Boat Plans at Mystic Seaport* (2000) focused on a few of these collections: work by Starling Burgess, L. Francis Herreshoff, Winthrop Warner, Fredrick Geiger, Louis Kromholz, and Albert Condon. These are just a few of the dozens of designers represented in the ships plans collection. Photographs and histories of the boats in the Museum's collection can be found in the new edition of *Mystic Seaport Watercraft*. If you can't find what you want here, contact the Ships Plans Division, where there are plenty more plans of skiffs, canoes, catboats, and motorboats, as well as fancy cruising yachts and sturdy schooners. If you have the urge to build a boat, there's a lifetime of opportunities in the Ships Plans Collection at Mystic Seaport.

87 BOAT DESIGNS

Decked Canoe Rob Roy Type by Searle & Company

11' 11" x 2' 3" x 12"   ca. 1872

Accession No. 1958.1286
Catalog No. 7.104

Take off and lines by Robert A. Pittaway,
November 1975

Dozens of derivative designs, built in everything from mechanically fastened wood to rotomolded plastic, are called Rob Roys. This is the real thing, the fifth or seventh decked, double-paddle canoe built for John "Rob Roy" MacGregor, who began the canoe craze with an account of his 1865 canoe trip through Europe. MacGregor used this one to cruise in the Orkney and Shetland Islands of Scotland in 1872.

She is an example of the best English boatbuilding: great attention to lining out, fine proportion of parts, and decorative beads inside the coaming, on the top of the keel, and on the outside of the mahogany sheerstrake. Her lines are subtle, a bit finer forward than aft. She is not as flat floored as some of the modern variations. The Searle Company planked her with five planks of 1/4" oak, finishing with a mahogany sheerstrake. A little tumblehome at the sheerstrake makes paddling easier. There is no rudder; since the footbraces are solid, she probably never had one. She is fastened with clenched copper tacks in the scarfs and the laps, with rivets at the seven sawn, jogged frames and the two big floor timbers in ends. Eight sawn floor timbers spaced in between the frames support two to three planks. Deck panels are of 1/4" mahogany with 3/8" at the sides. These are single wide boards with an easy curve.

This design would adapt easily to glued-lapstrake construction. Most small canoes that are glue-lapped are planked with seven planks, which is something the prospective builder might want to consider. A builder might also want to add watertight bulkheads aft of the cockpit and forward of the riser; leave at least six feet clear if you want to sleep in the boat the way MacGregor did. If she was decked in plywood, you'd need to add rubrails to cover the edges, and you might want to put in mast tubes as well to make it easier to step the rig.

The seat is missing so you'll need to design one. The simplest would be a shallow box with canvas on top and a low backrest. Although there is no sail plan, like MacGregor you might consider a two-masted rig with a total sail area of 60 square feet. Balanced or boomed standing lug sails, with 10 to 15 square feet in the mizzen, would be an appropriate rig.

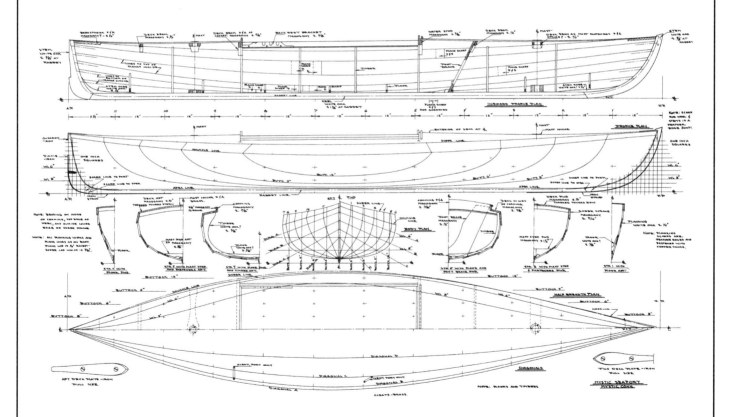

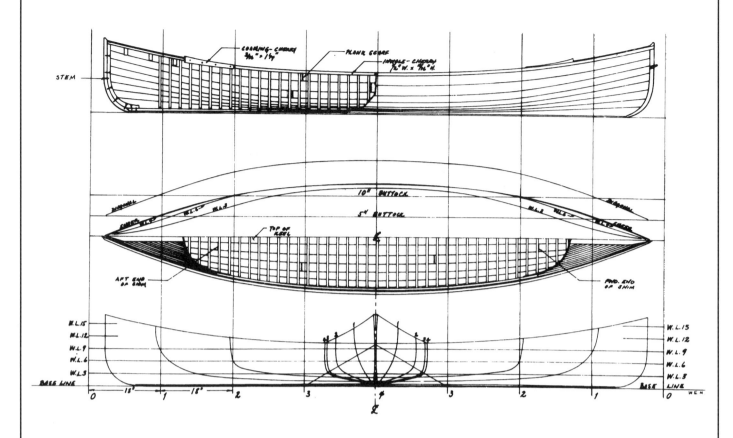

Decked Canoe by Rushton Vaux Jr. Model

11' 6" x 2' 2" x 10" ca. 1910
Catalog No. Misc. 26

Drawn by William E. Mills from lines taken off a loaned boat, March 1988

J. Henry Rushton of Canton, New York, responded to the small Rob Roy canoes with a series of double-paddle canoes built initially for George Washington Sears—"Nessmuk"—who wrote about traveling in the Adirondacks. Most useful of these were the Vaux models, named for an American Canoe Association founder and author, C. Bowyer Vaux.

The Vaux was carried in the Rushton catalogs from 1903 to 1915. This model was a foot to 18" longer than the Nessmuks. The Vaux and Vaux Jr. are the final evolution of Rushton's various double-paddle designs. Rushton's 1915 catalog noted that the 40-pound Vaux

model was a bit slower, but steadier, than the Arkansas Traveler, remarking: "it attracts considerable attention on account of its character, design and beautiful finish. Its lightweight makes it portable and an easy paddler. . . . Many Vauxs are used as errand canoes on houseboats, sailing boats and small motor boats. They are used extensively around New York City, because their length and breadth is so well proportioned that they keep exceptionally dry in rough water."

The boat is perfectly double-ended. A relatively hard-bilged, shallow V bottom should give some stability in this light boat. Eight planks to the side help get around the hard bilge. These are of 1/4" cedar with a guideboat lap, half-round elm frames spaced at 2 1/4" providing support. Instead of a thwart, 1/2" cherry inwales, and a rubrail that tapers from the stems out to 11/16" amidships, gives the boat athwartships rigidity. A builder might add a thwart and lighten the rails. Especially interesting is the typical Rushton garboard shim. Instead of cutting a shim for each frame to support the garboard, Rushton commonly used a

shim plank that ran three-quarters of the length of the boat. Typical of Rushton construction, the decks are edge-nailed 1/4" Spanish cedar, which is used for the sheerstrake as well. Rushton's catalog shows a floorboard and backrest, although these were not with this boat when it was measured.

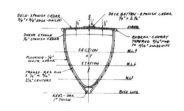

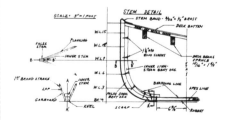

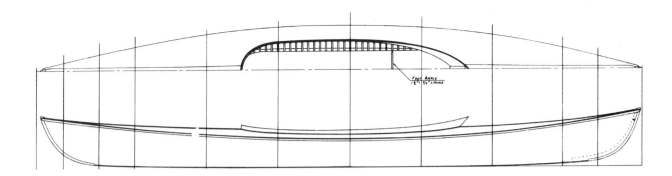

Chic
Decked Canoe

16′ 10″ x 2′ 4″ x 10″ ca. 1900

Accession No. 1961.262
Catalog No. 7.110

Drawing by William E. Mills,
from lines taken off June 1982

Atypical American double-paddle canoe a couple of generations

removed from the original Rob Roy, *Chic* would be a seaworthy flyer with her sheltering decks and relatively small cockpit. Her maximum width is six inches forward of amidships, but her forward sections are sharper than aft, promising decent speed. With her stem about two inches higher than her stern, she has a pleasing sheer.

Chic was built with 1/4″ cedar for her six-plank sides and 1/4″ bent elm frames on 2″ centers. Her lapstrake

planking is fastened with copper clench nails. The deck has a 3/16″ mahogany center strip covering the joint between the 3/16″ Spanish cedar deck planks. As in the Rob Roy, the deck and sides are supported by six spruce knees. *Chic* has a footbrace and presumably was fitted with a removable seat and back that are no longer with the boat. The plans include the floorboard. Today, inflated buoyancy bags could take the place of the soldered copper flotation tanks.

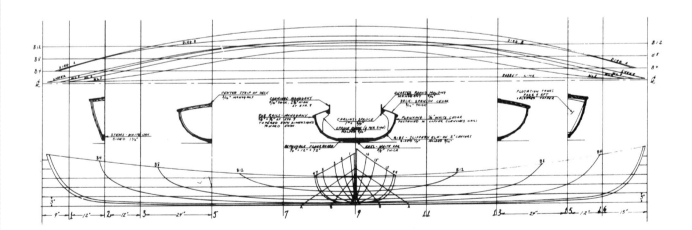

Open Canoe
by J. R. Robertson

15′ 0″ x 2′ 6″ x 10″ ca. 1900

Catalog No. Misc. 39

Highly detailed drawing by David W. Dillion, April 1991, from lines taken off a loaned canoe in November 1986

It is quite possible that canoe-builder J.R. Robertson of Auburndale, Massachusetts, learned his skills at the Rushton shop. He was born in Rushton's hometown of Canton, New York, and he lifted the contents of his first catalog directly from Rushton's in 1884. With its plumb stems and 15′ x 30″ proportions, this canoe is similar to the popular Canadian canoes from the shops around Peterborough, Ontario, introduced to American canoeists in the 1880s. It probably was built before 1903, when Robertson went to work with Old Town and later returned to Auburndale to convert his own production to wood-canvas. By 1905, Robertson could report: "the demand for this style has steadily decreased until they are almost a thing of the past and hereafter this type will be built to order only."

These plans have lots of information for the builder, including how to set up the rolling bevel needed on the stem rabbet. Lines and offsets are to inside corners of the planks. The boat has seven 1/4″ cedar planks, with 1/4″ x 9/16″ frames and a symmetrical hull. It is set up for one paddler and a passenger. A builder wanting to paddle it alone might choose to add a thwart just aft of amidships. For two paddlers, you might want to shift the after seat a bit farther aft.

Today, a builder might choose to use strip-planked or glued-lapstrake construction, both of which would produce a lighter boat, but it would not be as much of a head-turner as this cedar-planked one. No matter how built, she'd have the advantage of being faster than almost any stock 15′ open canoe on the market today, most of which are beamier.

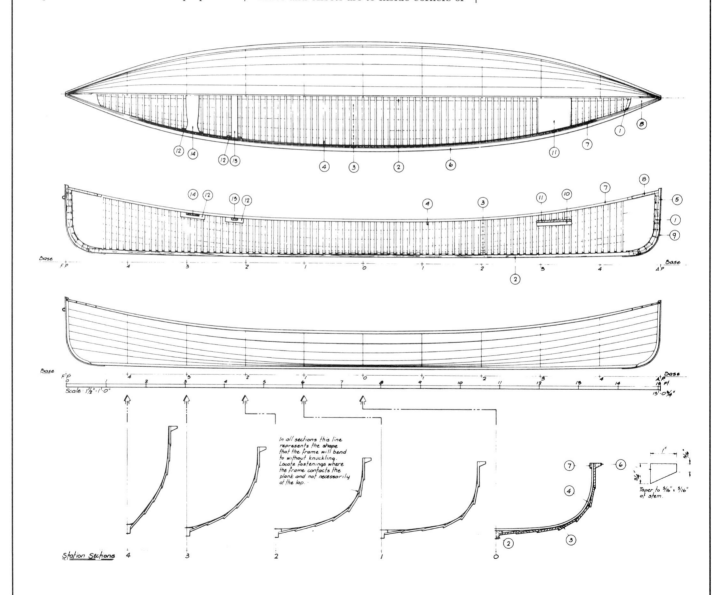

Rushton's Ugo and Arkansaw Traveler models, originally built between 1903 and 1915, would be fine choices for any builder looking for fast, elegant craft. Rushton was unique among canoe-builders in using the guideboat lap to create his smooth-skin canoes. A builder wanting to do an authentic job would use 1/4" cedar planking, with 1/4" Spanish cedar in the sheerstrake and tiny 1/4" x 1/2" elm frames spaced on 2 1/2" centers. The plans fully detail the backbones and all plank widths.

The challenge would be choosing the model. According to Rushton's catalog, the slim, fast Arkansaw Traveler "is not built like a racing shell, but at the same time it is fast enough to be in a class with them." This is perhaps a slight exaggeration, as is the suggestion: "when you take one out for a paddle be sure your hair is parted in the middle." The Ugo is a bit beamier and slightly flatter in the floors. The Rushton catalog noted: "It has moderate dead rise, quick bilge, fine lines, carries a heavy load with wonderful stiffness and is swift and easy under paddle."

For a discussion of traditional building techniques, see Chapter 6 of John Gardner's *More Building Classic Small Craft*, in which he examines and provides some drawings of Mystic's *Iola*, a 17' Arkansaw Traveler. With its seats and the full-length shim over the garboard, the Adirondack Museum boat weighs 62 pounds, which is a bit heavier than the "40 pounds and upward" claimed in Rushton's catalog. Of course, either boat would lend itself readily to strip-planked construction.

"Arkansaw" Traveler Model

16' 0" x 2' 5" x 11" ca. 1910

Catalog No. Misc. 32 (Adirondack Museum 60.44)

Drawn by David W. Dillion, May 1984

Ugo Model

16' 0" x 2' 6" x 11" ca. 1910

Catalog No. Misc. 34

Drawn by David W. Dillion, based on the hull of the Adirondack Museum's Nomad sailing canoe (60.43.1), which used the Ugo hull as a basis

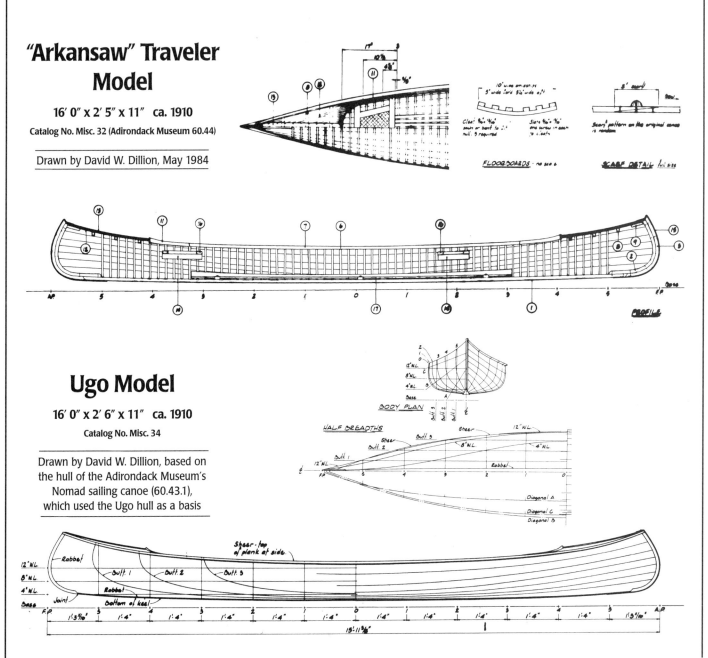

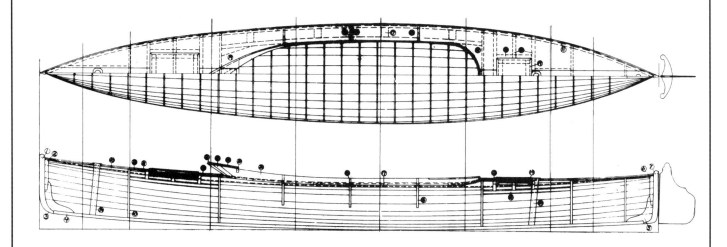

Sailing Canoe by William F. Wiser

14′ 6″ x 2′ 3″ x 1′ 3″ 1883

Catalog No. Misc. 20

Drawn by Ned B. Costello, March 1977

Mystic Seaport staff members ran across this boat in Belfast, Maine, in the 1970s. They got permission to measure her, and John Gardner's assistant, Ned Costello, drew her up. She was built by William F. Wiser of Bridesburg, Pennsylvania, who was an active builder in the 1880s. He ran a one-man shop, moving upriver from Philadelphia to Bridesburg sometime after 1880. His customers were members of canoe clubs like the Red Dragon, which moved to Bridesburg in 1890 after losing two clubhouses to fire at Cooper's Point in Camden, New Jersey.

This canoe is smaller than most sailing canoes of the time, and it would be a better paddler than the larger canoes. With her well-rockered keel, she would tack easily, which is something not all canoes of this era could do. Her Radix centerboard—a brass fan—folds nearly flat, allowing the skipper to sleep in the cockpit, while the watertight bulkheads keep gear dry and would keep the boat afloat if swamped. The plans have exceptionally useful isometric drawings of the decking.

This boat had no rig when measured. Ned Costello researched and adapted an appropriate rig from Dixon Kemp's 1886 *Manual of Yacht and Boat Sailing.* Radix centerboards are back in production, as is the rest of the hardware needed to build this boat. A sailing canoe like this would make a dandy cruiser for rivers and estuaries.

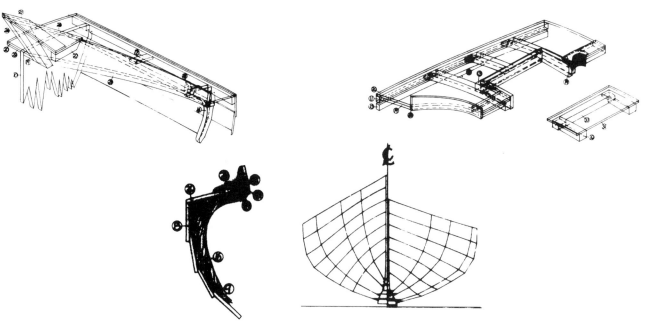

Skiff by Palmer

10' 0" x 4' 1"

Accession No. 1996.82

Measured by Robert Allingham and
Roger Hughes, May 1996,
and drawn by Roger Hughes

There was always a strong market for small skiffs. The Palmer Company of Cos Cob, Connecticut, got its start in 1895 when Frank and Ray Palmer installed their first production engine in a 15' Whitehall. By the 1930s their company was one of the nation's leading builders of marine engines. In the early days the Palmers contracted with nearby boatbuilders to produce boats in which

to install their engines, and they marketed complete packages under the Palmer name. Far too small for an engine, this skiff may have been sold as a tender for larger boats.

The boat has three planks per side and a cross-planked bottom, all constructed of 5/8" stock, probably cedar. The plan has all you need to shape the boat: plank widths for the bottom, dimensions for a mold amidships, and a transom pattern. The seat supports are unusually elegant for such a small skiff and provide substantial strength. She has a single center rowing station, which would make it hard to carry a single passenger; a removable seat resting on the top of the garboard up forward would help.

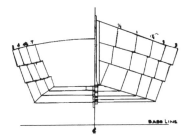

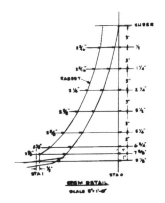

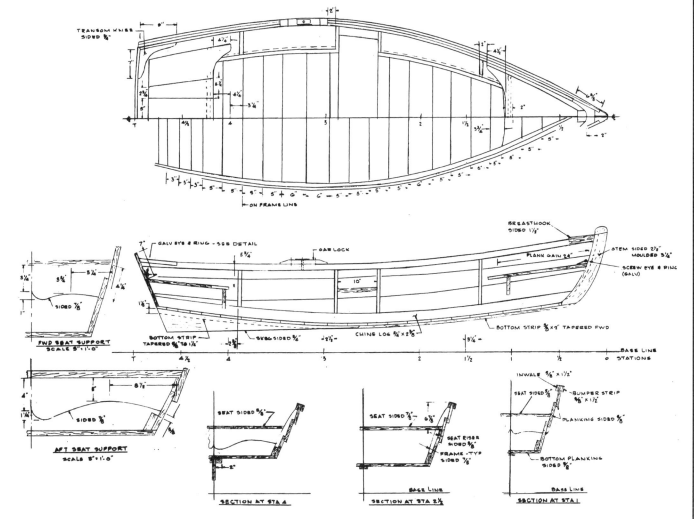

Wilbur
Flatiron Skiff

10′ 3″ x 3′ 9″

Accession No. 1976.72
Catalog No. 7.92

Drawn by Valerie Danforth, May 1978;
sail plan, October 1979

Around the waterfront, few boats are handier than a small flatiron skiff. This one is based on a classic in the Mystic Seaport collection, a 10-footer of unknown origin donated by Ned Ackerman. A near duplicate was built in 1977 by students in the Williams College-Mystic Seaport Maritime Studies Program, under the supervision of John Gardner and his assistant at the time, Val Danforth. It was such a nice boat that Val Danforth drew up what they had done. The boat would make a fine work skiff, a yacht tender, or a boat to turn a 10- or 50-year-old loose.

Wilbur, as one that stayed at the Museum before being sold was called, is a cross-planked skiff with two planks per side. She has a two-part stem for ease of construction. The plans are especially easy for amateur builders to interpret. John and Val gave the boat a daggerboard and a small spritsail to add to the fun. Her rocker is such that she would row pretty well, with two rowing stations so you can carry a passenger. Her external sternpost would present a bit of a problem if you wanted to use a small outboard motor. Judicious use of cheek pieces was the usual way to allow for the attachment of an outboard. The post also means that a sculling notch would need to be set off to one side. The port side is usual for a right-hander, so that the sculler can face forward while gripping the oar across the front of her body, using the whole body to push the boat along.

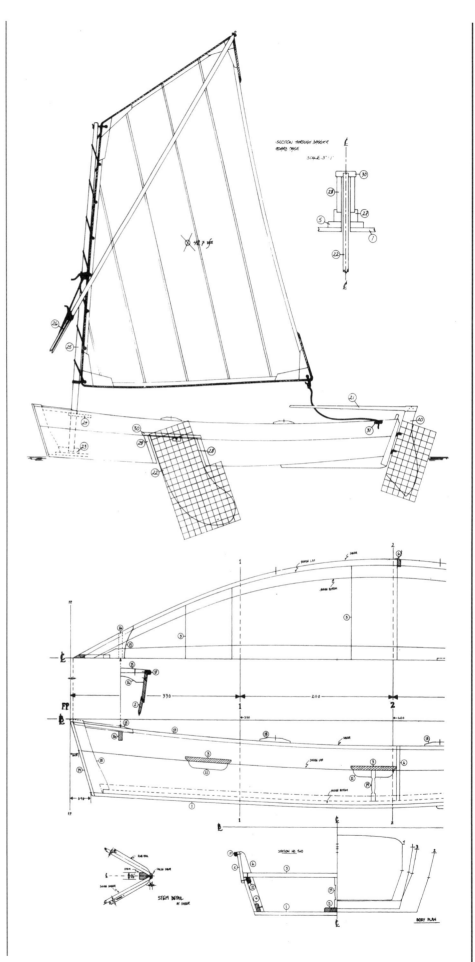

Skiff from New Bedford, Massachusetts, by Asa Thomson

11' 2" x 4' 3"   1927

Accession No. 1976.148
Catalog No. 7.95

Offsets by Dan Phalen; scantlings by Maynard Bray, 1979; drawn by Spencer Lincoln, May 1979

The plans for the Asa Thomson skiff are a result of a collaboration with *WoodenBoat* magazine, which got Spencer Lincoln to draw the boat. *WoodenBoat* also carries these plans, as well as plans for a larger version called a Yankee Tender.

Flatiron skiffs don't come any fancier than this. Asa Thomson, a New Bedford boatbuilder, built this one in 1927, some 42 years after he set up his shop. Her double bottom is unique, allowing her to dry out without leaking when going back overboard. She has an external keel rather than the internal keelson found on many skiffs, which makes her easy to bail and clean out. This particular one even has a fish or bait well under the center seat. This structure keeps the boat from needing the seat knees that Thomson put on his regular skiffs.

Asa called these his skiff-tenders. He kept them light, under 100 pounds, or about two-thirds the weight of a normal flatiron skiff of this size. The considerable rocker keeps the transom out of the water even with three aboard. Her unusually high sides would keep out the Buzzards Bay chop. At a cost of $140, and charging a day rate of $1.25, Thomson put at least 80 hours into one of these skiffs—perhaps twice that needed in a simple flatiron—and the workmanship shows it.

For more information on this boat, see Dan Phalen's "Asa Thomson's Elegant Skiffs," *WoodenBoat* 29, July/August 1979.

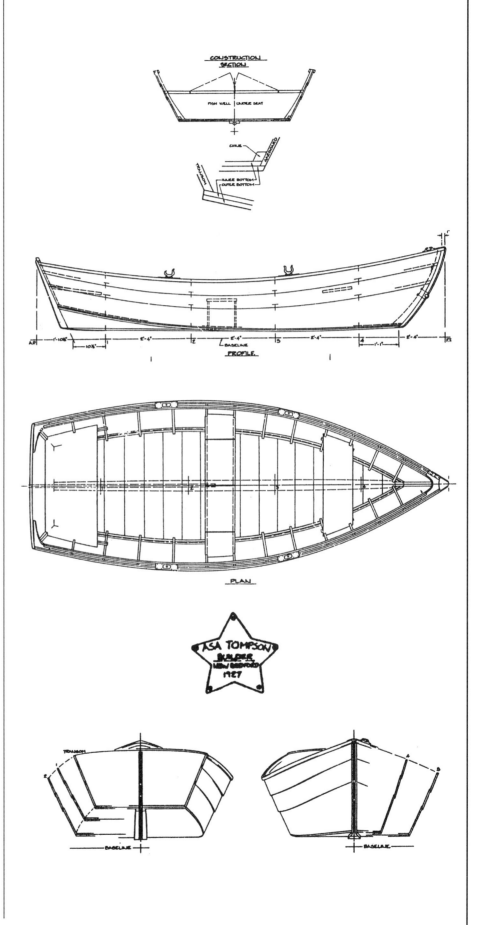

L ocal to the Mystic River area of eastern Connecticut were flatiron skiffs called Noank Skiffs or Noank Sharpies. Compared to other flatiron skiffs, these have a little less flare than most. Relatively vertical sides allow the seats to rest on top of the lower plank. In the many built without chines, the cross-planked bottoms were nailed right into the side planks. Repairs often included adding chine logs. Here are three of these simple, handy skiffs from which to choose.

Noank Sharpie-Skiff

12′0″ x 4″   ca. 1950

Catalog No. Misc. 42

Drawn by Lawrence Jacobsen, July 1996

T he 12′ sharpie-skiff was built near the mouth of the Mystic River at Noank by Robert Whittaker to a Jerry Davis design. Chine logs were added later during repairs, as were cheek pieces in the transom. She has a shallow runner forward to assist when hauling onto a float or ramp.

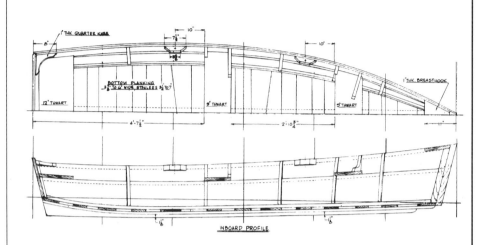

Noank Sharpie-Skiff

12′ 6″ x 4′ 4″

Catalog No. Misc. 8

Drawn by Robert A. Pittaway, September 1974

T he largest of the Noank skiffs was owned by Mystic Seaport employee and Noank native Arnold Crossman when Rob Pittaway measured her. She was a bit fancy with a beaded sheer strake and unlike the others did not have a chine log repair. She has a bit too much rise in the stern to make her well suited for an outboard.

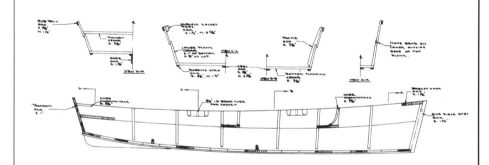

Noank Sharpie-Skiff

12′ 3″ x 4′ 6″   ca. 1950

Catalog No. Misc. 43

Drawn by Lawrence Jacobsen, ca. 1950

T he 12′ 3″ boat was built at Noank by Webster Eldredge. The chine logs were added when the boat was repaired by Robert Whittaker.

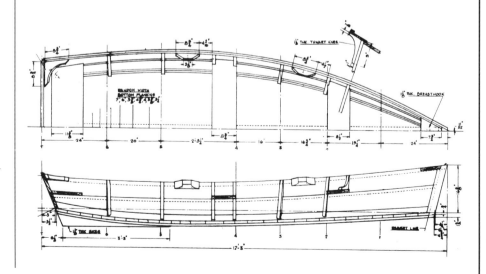

Riverfront Recapture Sharpie-Skiff

13' 9" x 4' 0"   1988

Catalog No. Misc. 38

Drawn by John Gardner, June 1988

In June 1988, John Gardner designed the 13' 9" Riverfront Recapture sharpie-skiff to be built as part of a youth program in Hartford, Connecticut. The plan includes directions for the building form as well as expansions for the single-piece plywood sides. Modest rocker means that the boat rows well, but a light outboard could also be fitted.

Besides the plans, a 20-page instruction booklet is available for this easy-to-build boat. More information on the boat is in Chapter 2 of John Gardner's *Classic Small Craft You Can Build.*

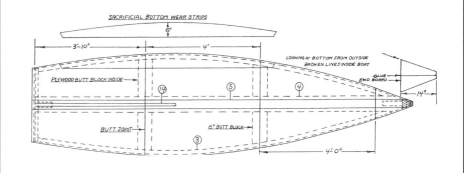

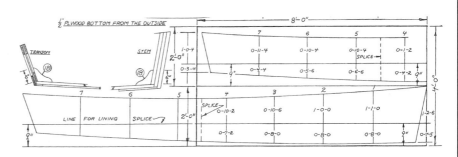

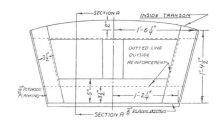

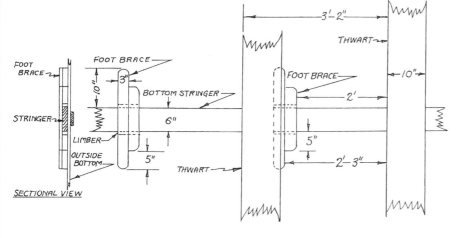

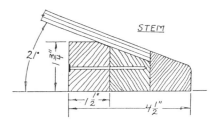

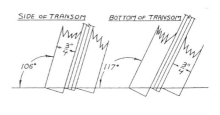

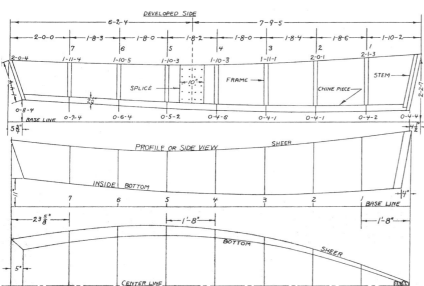

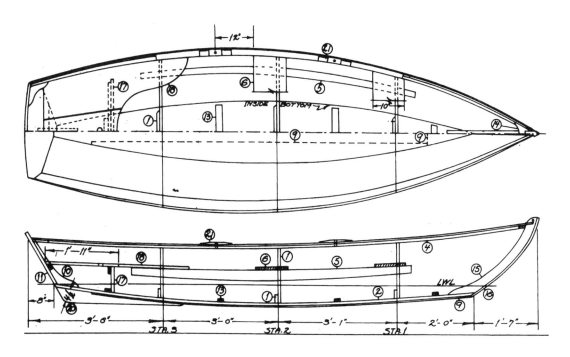

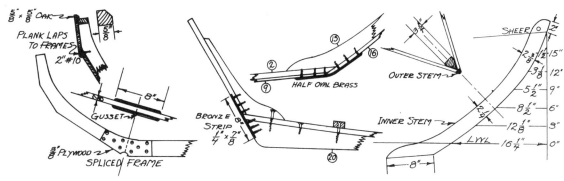

Dory-Skiff by Chamberlain

13' 5" x 4' 0"

Accession No. 1971.238
Catalog No. 7.32

Drawn by Robert A. Pittaway, January 1974

This 13' Chamberlain dory-skiff is hard to beat for a seaworthy small boat under 14'. It performs far better in open water than does a flatiron skiff. Dory-skiffs are as good as or better than round-bottom boats for the same purpose, and they are much easier to build. As an additional benefit, with their narrow flat bottom they remain level when beached.

This dory-skiff's narrow stern and entry mean easy motion and speed under oar. But the transom is too fine at the water-

line to stand an outboard, even a small one. Most of the original builders of these small dories used three narrow planks below the knuckle at the turn of the bilge, since wide stock was hard to come by and was prone to checking after some years of use. Today we might use plywood for this strake, as well as for the bottom, then continue planking above the first turn with grown wood.

Rob Pittaway worked up these lines from dimensions taken by John Gardner from patterns, and he added a nice low-aspect-ratio sloop rig of 83 square feet, which adds to the boat's versatility. The penalty would be losing the forward rowing station, which is needed when rowing with a passenger. At Mystic Seaport's Boathouse boat livery, *Harry Williams*—the first boat built in the Museum's boat shop in 1971—has been highly popular. After the 2001 season, *Harry Williams* was retired and a

replacement was built to keep this popular and practical model in the livery fleet. In 1986, one of these Chamberlains was given to the collection; she has proven to be a few inches different from the design based on patterns.

For more information see Sharon Brown's articles in the 1 and 15 October 2001 issues of *Messing About in Boats*, and Chapter 25 in John Gardner's *Dory Book*, which includes a redrawn version.

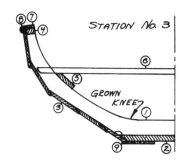

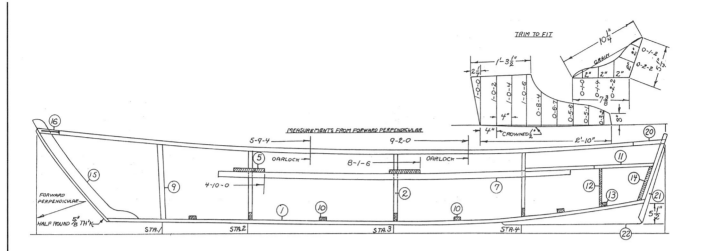

Amesbury Dory-Skiff by Lancaster

13′ 6″ x 4′ 0″   1924

Accession No. 1989.94.1
Catalog No. 112.18

Measured and drawn by John Gardner,
October 1989

John Gardner drew this dory-skiff shortly after she arrived at Mystic

Seaport. Built by C.H. Lancaster of Amesbury, Massachusetts, in 1924, she was used for about 25 years as a family lake fishing boat. She is slightly larger than the Chamberlain dory-skiff: her bottom is about 6″ wider and her sides are straighter as well, with only a slight knuckle at the first bend. At rest, or when you jump in and out, she would be a little steadier than the Chamberlain—somewhat more akin to a flatiron skiff—but not as easy as the

Chamberlain in the rollers and slower under oar. Her three-part stern bench has a removable center section, which is a good idea in these little boats, where it is sometimes hard to tuck things underneath the seat and to reach during spring painting. With a fairly vertical transom and wide stern, she will take an outboard motor.

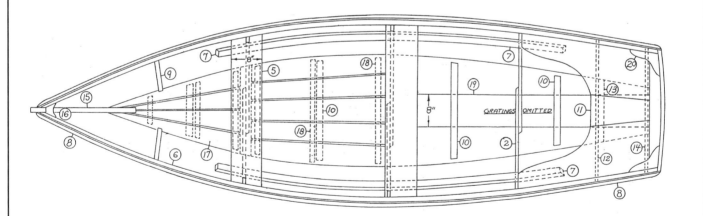

Marblehead Dory-Skiff

14′ 0″ x 4′ 5″ ca. 1976

Catalog No. Misc. 18

Drawn by Alison H. Pyott, December 1976

This Marblehead dory-skiff was designed by John Gardner as an expansion of the Chamberlain that was the first project in the Mystic Seaport boat shop. Gardner lengthened the boat to 14′ and gave it more beam generally, and specifically aft above the waterline, to improve sailing qualities. John's assistant, Alison Pyott, drew up the boat as it would have been built traditionally: start with a carved half model and build to the usual practice. *Morsel*, the first of five Marblehead dory-skiffs built in the shop, has returned to the Museum after three owners (all Mystic Seaport staff members) and is now at the Museum's Boathouse boat livery.

Morsel is sized well for the single rower, though she's a bit small for a pair, and she makes a nice, forgiving sailboat for a couple of adults and a child. Her long dinghy-style side benches, where you can sit to windward while staying dry, make sailing easy. The modest spritsail sloop rig provides plenty of area for summer breezes and has a set of reef points for those days of small craft warnings. Builders have suggested that battens are not needed in the sail and have noted that, when single-handing, the overlapping jib hangs on the end of the sprit when tacking. It would not be hard to redesign the rig for a single sail, moving the forward thwart forward some and the centerboard aft. Just keep the same relative position of the centers of resistance and effort. The rudder can come out of the water, heeling in a seaway; a hiking stick that lets the sailor get to windward, or an old-fashioned steering yoke, would let the boat be sailed flatter. There is even enough space forward of the mast for a youngster to act as lookout and figurehead.

Plans call for 1/2″ white pine or cedar planking with a 7/8″ bottom. If the builder wanted to use plywood, it would be well to drop 1/16″ in thickness, as plywood is generally heavier than similar-sized natural wood. Besides materials, the plans provide a full fastening schedule.

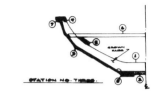

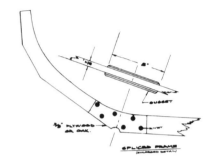

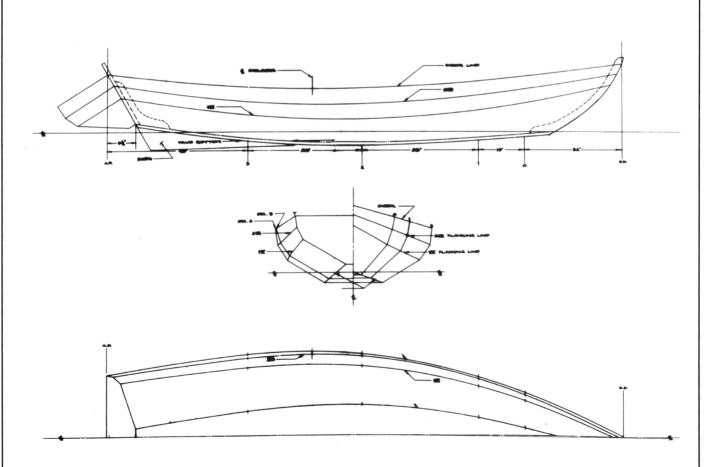

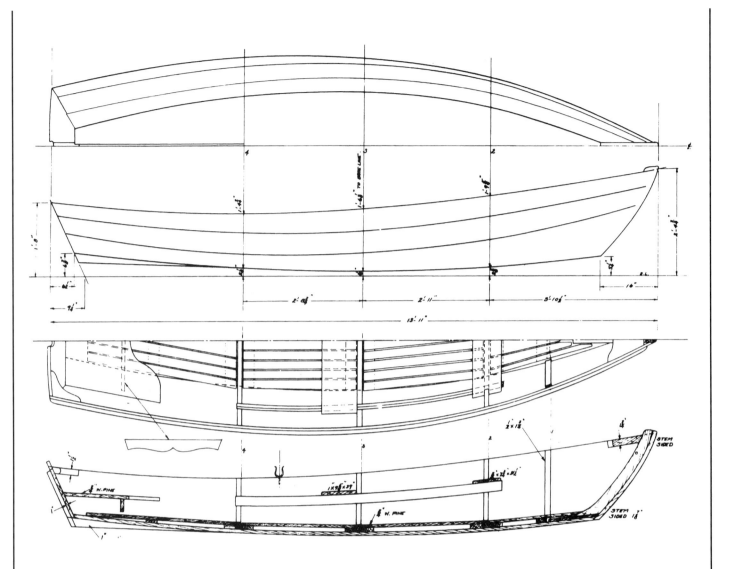

Amesbury Dory-Skiff

14′ 0″ x 4″ 0″ ca. 1930

Accession No. 1957.290
Catalog No. 7.24

Drawn by Edson I. Schock

This dory-skiff may well have been built at the Lowell dory shop in Amesbury as one of the boats produced when the shop turned to the recreational market in the years after dory fishing peaked. She is shallower than the Lancaster dory-skiff, with a slightly narrower bottom and a bit more sheer. With barely any knuckle in the sides at all—just a few degrees at the sheerstrake—her shape is more like a flatiron skiff than the usual dory-skiff.

Her plans were drawn in the 1950s and are not as detailed as the Museum's later plans. The information needed is all there, except for the location of that knuckle, which must be scaled off the plans and may require some work with a batten to set sweetly. With a little less freeboard than the other dory-skiff selections, this boat would be a good choice for protected waters.

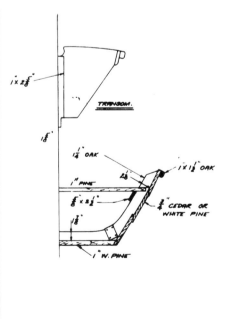

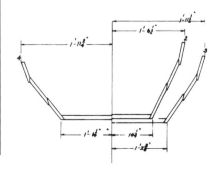

Piscataqua River Wherry

16' 5" x 4' 1"   ca. 1850

Accession No. 1973.236
Catalog No. 7.91

Drawn by Valerie Danforth,
September 1978 and April 1979

My rowing partner owns one of these, and I have spent hours in it single and double, summer and winter. She is a bit heavy for top speed with a single rower, but when you slack off a notch the boat covers ground fast. With two rowers up and cruising, she holds 4 to 4 1/2 knots easily, with a hull speed of about 5 knots. But this wherry was developed as a water taxi for one or two people to carry several, not as a racing machine. Racing variations stretched and built lightly have done well in traditional boat racing, beaten only by St. Lawrence River skiffs and Adirondack

guideboats. She'll certainly go as well as more complex boats of her same length and weight. But in winter, I like a little weight. Boarding over the bow from a snow-covered float into a boat that needs to be shoveled out, a little steadiness under foot and knee is desirable.

Like most skegless dories, she needs to be trimmed by the stern to keep her on course crosswind and downwind. Unless you carry passengers, you can do without the stern seat. For racing, we repositioned the bow seat aft one frame (to the bent frame) and the new stern seat aft four inches or so in order still to stay on its full frame. We moved the amidships seat (used in solo rowing) back a few inches, mirroring the stern seat shift, and we remove it when rowing double. Even with these adjustments in trim, she needs a bit of beach rock to get her to stay on course, especially solo. She was originally set up for thole pins on top of the gunwale; we put the after oarlocks

on the outside of the rubrail to match more closely our oar lengths when rowing double.

Val Danforth's clear, detailed plans show the small compartment under the stern sheets where the ferry man could keep lunch. The plans also include the 1/2" pine false bottom that protected the original boat from wear as an off-the-rocky-beach ferry. The plans also show a lighter scantling set used in the wherry built by the Williams College-Mystic Seaport Maritime Studies Program students at the Museum.

With its narrow flat bottom and the fair curves of its long, lean shape, this wherry builds easily, with only 8"-wide boards needed to lay out the planks. Others have found that she is easy to plank in plywood. If plywood is used, it would be well to drop a size from the grown plank scantlings in order to keep the weight down.

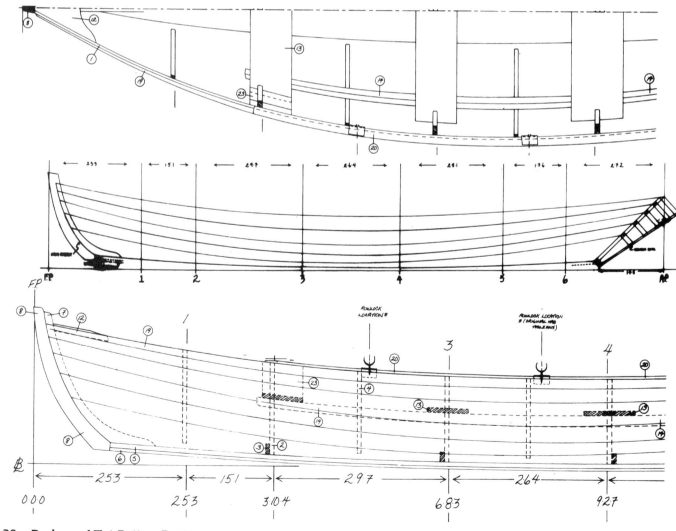

W.B.
New Haven
Sharpie-Skiff

15′ 9″ x 5′ 1″ ca. 1888

Accession No. 1951.4206
Catalog No. 7.65

Drawn by Edson I. Schock

A small sharpie-skiff makes a fine recreational sailboat, as the numerous modern variants of *W.B.* attest. They have been built both conventionally and in plywood and are available in kits as well as plans. For a sharpie-skiff with a pedigree, it is hard to do better than *W.B.*, built about 1888 for the children of one of New Haven's prominent oyster-bed (and sharpie) owners. Mystic Seaport's reproduction of *W.B.*, built by

Willets Ansel, is a favorite. She has three mast steps, so she can be sailed as a cat-ketch or a cat, like her big working sisters, the 20′ to 35′ oystering sharpies. Horizontal sprit booms tame the rig; the sails are often furled about the masts, and the reefs are vertical. There is plenty of space for a family of four, and there are enough strings to keep more than one busy operating the rig if desired. This sharpie-skiff is not the best for rowing, but with a 12′ sculling oar she would move well, and there is an oarlock socket aft to take one.

W.B. can come off the mooring, be sailed about the river, and make the mooring again, with the tiller lashed the entire time. The rudder shown on the plans does hang down below the bottom and does not kick up, so if you plan to beach the boat, you might want to build a kick-

up rudder. On the Museum's reproduction boat, Will Ansel trimmed off the top of the rudder, which does not do much work, so the rudder can be pulled up vertically. The Schock plans have enough information to build the boat, but you might want to consult John Gardner's *Building Classic Small Craft*, which has information on 18′ and 20′ sharpies.

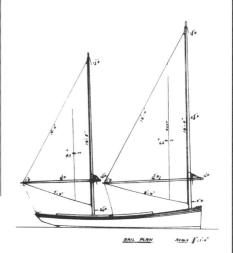

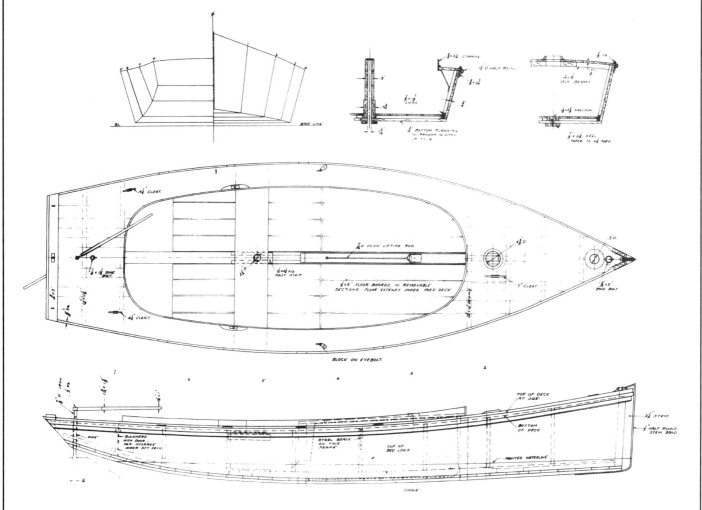

Swampscott Sailing Dory

17' 3" x 4' 6" 1974

Accession No. 1974.1025
Catalog No. 7.108

Drawn by Robert A. Pittaway, January 1975

You need a dorymate to get the best out of a 17' Swampscott dory. It is a big boat for one person to row quickly, and if there is any breeze you need some weight to windward under sail. With its fine stern, a Swampscott needs to be sailed from amidships. Traditionally a yoke-and-line steering system was used; now you might substitute a tiller and extension.

John Gardner modeled this boat, and Rob Pittaway drew up the results as

John built her with Barry Thomas in the Mystic Seaport boat shop in 1974. His plans give you the general plank shapes, call for thole pins for rowing, and include a false bottom to protect the planks when grounding. Three rowing positions let you balance the boat's trim. The sloop rig drawn by Rob is completely traditional, with no blocks or

cleats to ease sail handling. A 21st-century sailor without the calluses of a 19th-century Swampscott fisherman might want to modernize the rig. Big Swampscotts like this one have proven to be excellent family boats, with plenty to do for everyone, yet they are not so complex that they can't be operated solo.

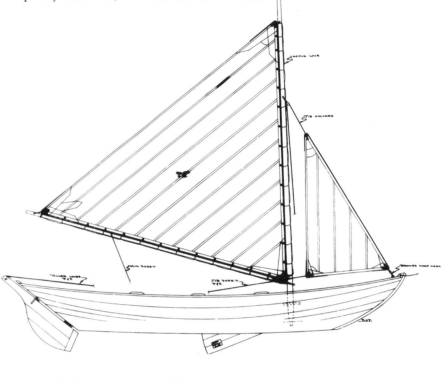

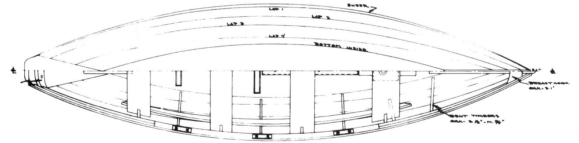

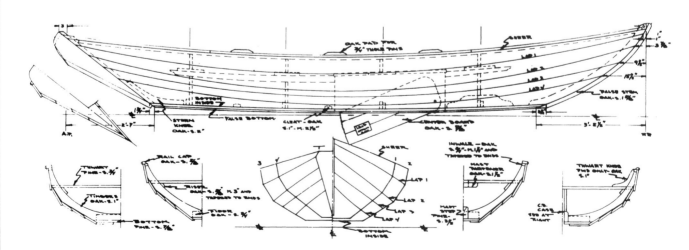

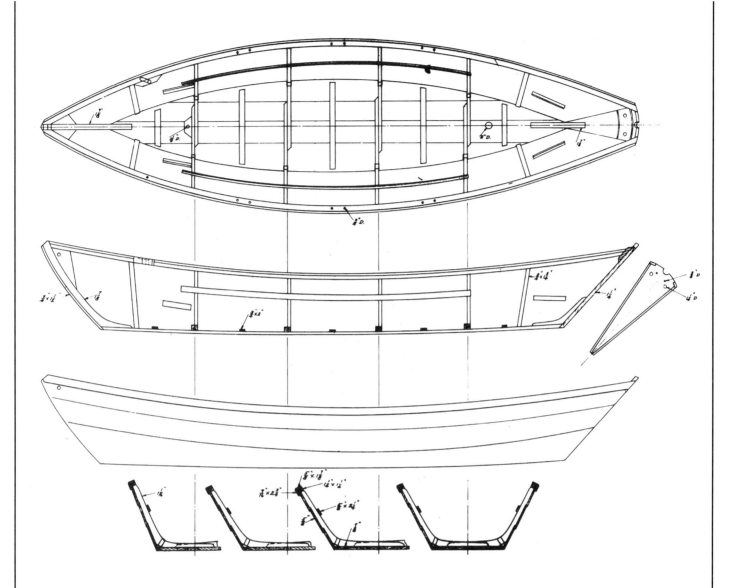

Banks Dory from the Schooner *Black Hawk*

18′ 3″ x 5′ 1″   ca. 1940

Accession No. 1955.320
Catalog No. 7.31

Drawn by Edson I. Schock

The converted schooner-yacht *Black Hawk* was possibly the last dory-fishing schooner to sail out of Connecticut, fishing in the 1940s and early 1950s. This two-man dory was one of her set of eight. These banks dories were serious work tools and are not really as well suited for recreation as are the lighter, round-bilged Swampscott types. However, with their straight sides, banks dories are easier to build. They are steady with a load, but they feel somewhat tender to the novice when light. They have been known to toss novice dory racers overboard in the heat of a 180° turn. Wider-bottom models are more stable when light, but are slower under oar.

Mystic Seaport has plans for three banks dories. Besides this one there is a 20′ model (1970.686), and a smaller 17′ Massachusetts Humane Society dory with steam-bent frames rather than the usual sawn frames, which was used at the Siasconset, Nantucket, Life-Saving Station (1963.1517).

On McGee Island, along the coast of Maine, sits a boathouse full of wooden boats. Most of them were brought up from the Swampscott area of Massachusetts as a fleet for a new summer home in the early 1900s. A Mystic Seaport crew was invited out to the island to document some of the boats in June 1983. Without much time to work, we had to be selective. Four outstanding boats were measured and drawn by John Gardner and Bill Mills. I held the tape, wrote things down, and took pictures. All the boats were of interest, but these four offer special possibilities for prospective builders.

Fat Boat
Dory-Skiff
by Gardner

12' 6" x 5' 0"   ca. 1910

Catalog No. Misc. 23

Drawn by John Gardner, 1983

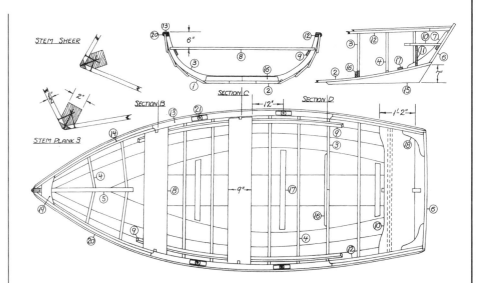

The smallest of the McGee Island boats is the one the family called *Fat Boat*. She is a chunky utility dory-skiff 12' 6" by 5'. She swallowed four of us, duffel, John's toolbox, and our pattern stock supply without coming close to being overloaded, and she still rowed well. Later, three of us went out in her to lift and shift some granite moorings by using tight pennants and rolling the boat.

John drew her up as Guy Gardner of Swampscott (one of George Chaisson's competitors) built her. He then redrew the plans to 13' 7", adding a sailing rig and glued-lapstrake plywood construction, describing her fully in Chapter 8 of his *Wooden Boats to Build and Use*.

Dory-Skiff
by Chaisson

14' 5" x 4' 4"   ca. 1920

Catalog No. Misc. 27

Drawn by William E. Mills, July-August 1983

Next in size on McGee Island is a 14' 5" Chaisson-built dory-skiff, which is unusual in having fore, aft, and side decks. It's a handsome boat, with the decks providing additional security in the open waters of Muscongus Bay. While this boat would do well with a sailing rig, she does not have one, though some smaller dory-skiffs did. This plan would be handy if one were thinking of decking another dory-skiff or wanted a boat to which a sailing rig could be added.

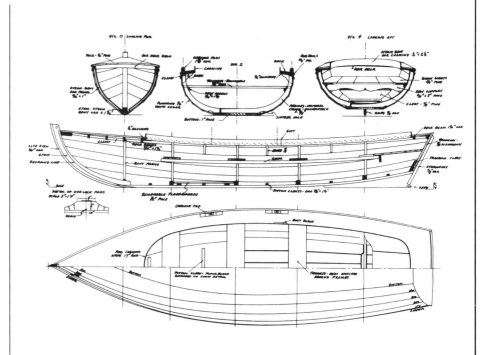

A Light Dory

17' 11" x 4' 5"   ca. 1915

Catalog No. Misc. 3

Drawn by William E. Mills, June 1983

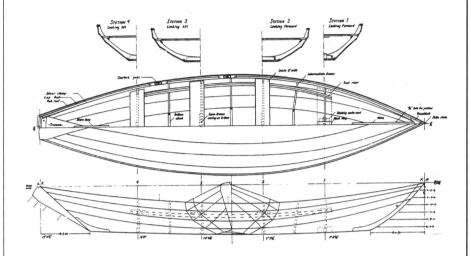

A lovely 18' light dory by an unknown builder caught our eyes. Her 3/8" pine planking is lighter than that of any of the gunning dories that John Gardner documented, and she is lower and leaner too. She'd be a flyer under oars. Her rowing positions would let her trim by the stern with a single rower, and about level with two. Under some conditions, she would need a bit of weight in the stern. A mast step would allow a small sail to be set to help the run home. She was painted olive drab, so she may have been intended for winter eider hunting.

Swampscott Dory by Chaisson

21' 4" x 4' 6"   ca. 1915

Catalog No. Misc. 28

Drawn by William E. Mills, September 1983

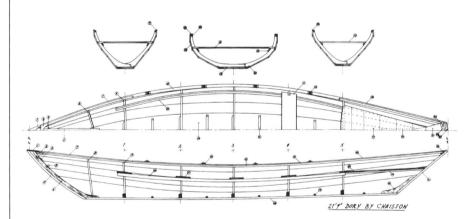

21'4" DORY BY CHAISSON

The final boat we measured on McGee Island was a 21' rowing Swampscott dory by Chaisson. She was one of the fanciest dories that John Gardner had ever seen, with a stern that had been hollowed out for looks, and beads (not included on the plans) on the inside edges of the planks as well as on the sheerstrake. She was set up with four rowing stations, but when we tried the replica built some years later, the boat was overpowered with four adults rowing. She'd be something with four youngsters and a coxswain. Originally, she was probably rowed by two or three, with the extra station providing some flexibility in trimming the boat.

We set up a replica with three rowing stations, leaving the amidships bench fixed. The forward one was moved aft a bit; the second station disappeared; and the after one slid aft with some short, fixed outriggers added, so that everyone could row the same length oars. A long, shallow skeg was added for tracking. Set up this way, she was a fast boat on the open-water racing circuit, with a couple of wins in the Blackburn races around Cape Ann to her credit. The garboard is a pretty wide board, and on the replica it checked under the stress of trailering and wetting and drying. If you decide to build this boat, it might be better to use plywood for the garboard or to use two narrow planks.

Madelon
Yacht Tender
by Lawley

9′ 3″ x 3′ 8″ ca. 1920

Accession No. 1977.254
Catalog No. 7.90

Drawn by Julia Rabinowitz, September 1978

With their fine lines and delicate construction, yacht tenders represent the highest art of production boat-building. And *Madelon* is a classic example, built by George F. Lawley & Sons of Neponset, Massachusetts, one of the leading producers of elegant yachts and tenders. Julia Rabinowitz's plans do her justice, with lots of details such as plank widths and bevels, tapers to risers and the keel batten, and alternative stern and deadwood construction for someone who can't get the hackmatack crook used here. A fastening schedule is included as well.

At just 9′, she's small, without the side benches commonly found in 10′ and 12′ tenders that would carry four people.

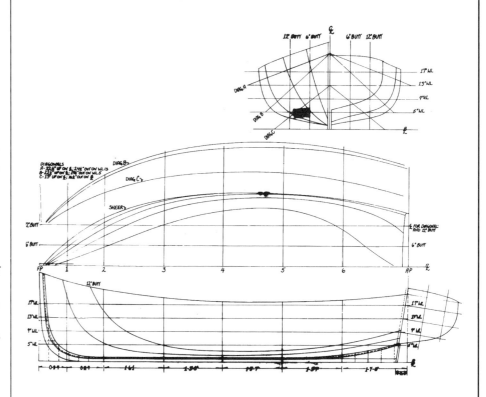

Three would be the maximum load, and two would be nicer. She'd look pretty handsome behind a small traditional sailing yacht; or she'd be an elegant substitute for a yacht. Studying this plan would help anyone interested in building fancy tenders, no matter the size, do a better job.

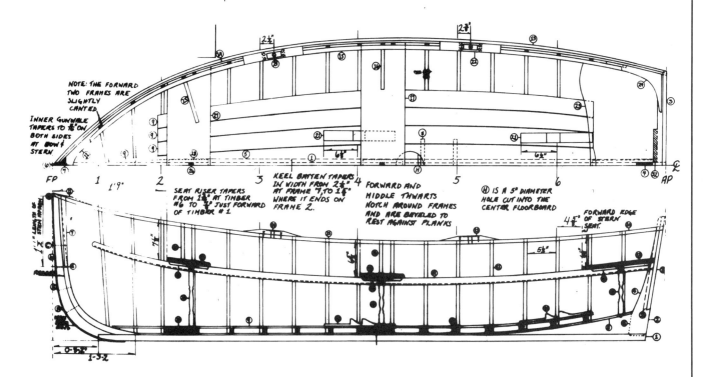

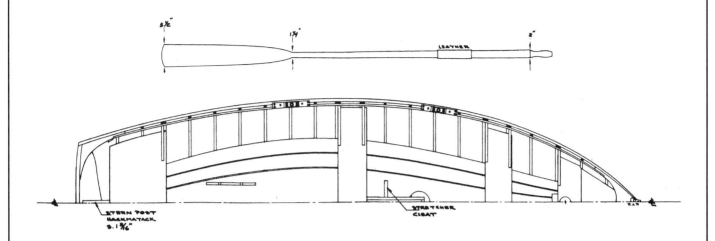

Herreshoff Dinghy

11' 6" x 4' 1" 1905

Accession No. 1974.930
Catalog No. 7.112

Drawn by Robert A. Pittaway, July 1975

Something like 50 boats were originally built to the design of this rowing and sailing dinghy, a smaller version of the ones that the Herreshoff Manufacturing Company built for the America's Cup contender *Columbia*. When Barry Thomas learned the Herreshoff techniques from Charlie Sylvester, one of the last of the

Herreshoff Manufacturing Company boatbuilders, and built a reproduction of this boat, he opened new paths in small-boat building at Mystic Seaport. It took Charlie Sylvester about 130 hours to build a slightly smaller boat; I wonder if we could do so well today.

For sailing, the Herreshoff dinghy has a daggerboard for efficiency and to minimize slot resistance under oars, with a fitted plug to fill the slot. A short tiller is used when you have a crew, a steering yoke and lines for solo sailing. Her spars are a little long to go in the boat when stowed. They'd need to be lashed or stowed aboard the mother ship if this

boat were to be used as a tender. As users of various replicas of this boat will attest, she is an ideal tender: capacious enough for four, and spritely under oar and sail. And the proud builder and owner would have a Herreshoff.

Rob Pittaway's plans are also published in Barry Thomas's little book, *Building the Herreshoff Dinghy: The Manufacturer's Method.* You should have both if you want to build this boat; and you should have Barry's book if you are thinking about lapstrake construction or any other Herreshoff project.

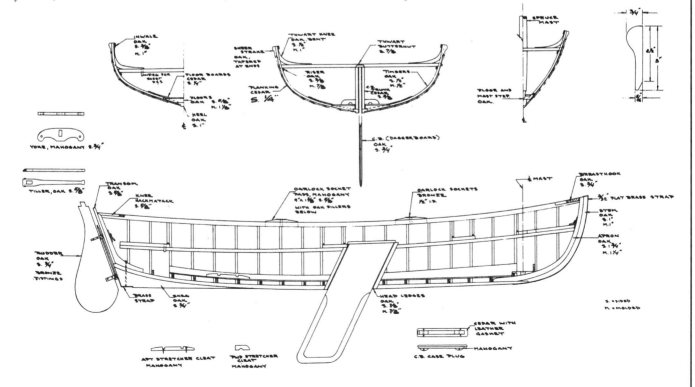

Heavy Duty Yacht Tender and Utility Boat

11' 10" x 4' 3" ca. 1925

Catalog No. Misc. 34

Drawn by John Gardner, 1986

This boat was Fred Dion's favorite tender. For 50 years, he operated a yacht yard in Salem, Massachusetts, which built tenders and took care of some of the North Shore's finest yachts.

It's likely that this boat was built in Maine. Besides being stouter all around than the better-known tenders by Lawley, Herreshoff, and others, she has a flatter floor and a harder turn to the bilge, and she does not have the wineglass stern found in many.

John Gardner devoted a chapter to this boat in *Wooden Boats to Build and Use*, recounting how Fred Dion and his nephew Rich rowed the boat out into the teeth of the Hurricane of 1938 to check mooring pennants. Working together on a single set of oars, they

made progress, and "the boat rode the waves like a duck, no solid water coming aboard." I'm not sure that I would want to be out on a day like that in any boat, and certainly not in one of the smaller fancy tenders. In 1990, Robert Dion gave Mystic Seaport a slightly smaller tender (1990.152) that was built at the Dion yard and was largely inspired by this boat.

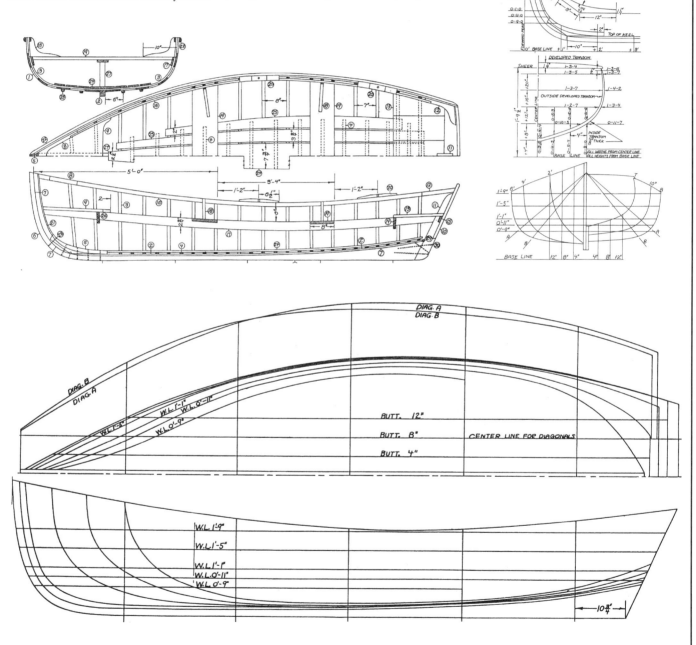

Whitehall-Type Sailboat

11′ 0″ x 4′ 1″

Accession No. 1973.22
Catalog No. 7.79

Drawn by Robert A. Pittaway,
December 1973; lines corrected and
redrawn by William E. Mills, 1983

This was a beautiful little boat. But when she came to Mystic Seaport she was a relic without deck or thwarts, although you could see where they went. Evidence for shallow seats and notches forward indicate that she may have had side decks and a foredeck to make up for her low freeboard, as did gunning boats such as the Seaford skiff, melonseed, sneakbox, and Delaware ducker. Her shape and construction put her in the Whitehall class. Rob Pittaway drew her up, as is, just after she arrived at the Museum, and he also drew a proposed sailing rig and deck reconstruction. Bill Mills relofted the plans about 10 years later. Rob's suggestions seem to have worked pretty well, according to at least one person I know who has built a boat to her plans. She would make a uniquely handsome small sailing craft for one, or maybe for two close friends.

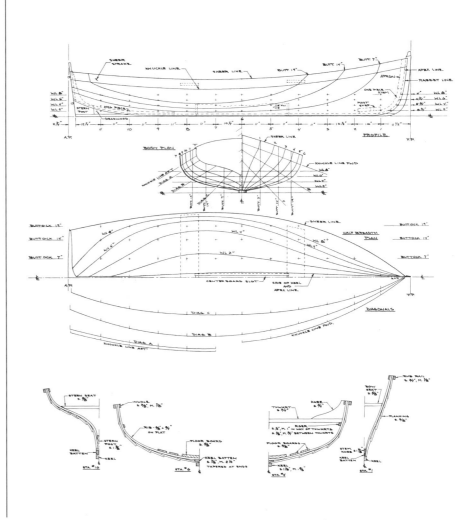

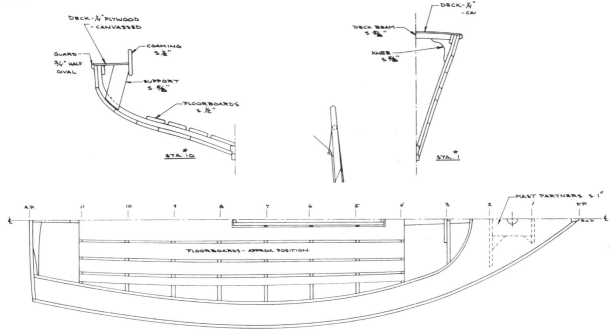

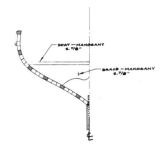

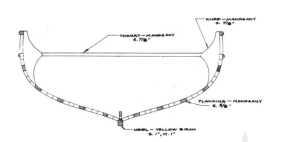

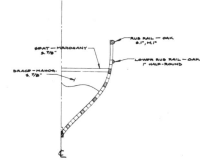

Favorite
Strip-Planked Whitehall-Style Pulling Boat

11′ 9″ x 4′ 0″   ca. 1900

Accession No. 1940.504
Catalog No. 7.35

Drawn by Alison H. Pyott, March 1976

Favorite was the fifth boat in Mystic Seaport's collection. She is strip-planked: fastened with nails in the 5/8" mahogany strips, which was not uncommon, especially in Maine about 1900. Her interior is mahogany like her planks, producing a substantial, 165-pound boat. Her keel—of yellow birch like her entire backbone—is not as straight as that of a pure Whitehall, curving up a bit for the forward third. As a pulling boat for one, she will cover a

mile in 20 minutes with moderate effort. Her sizable seat knees provide an excellent example of how to fasten seats into strip-planked boats with both strength and elegance. Strip construction also allows her to have a touch of tumblehome aft. With today's glues for strip-plank construction, she'd be a fine project.

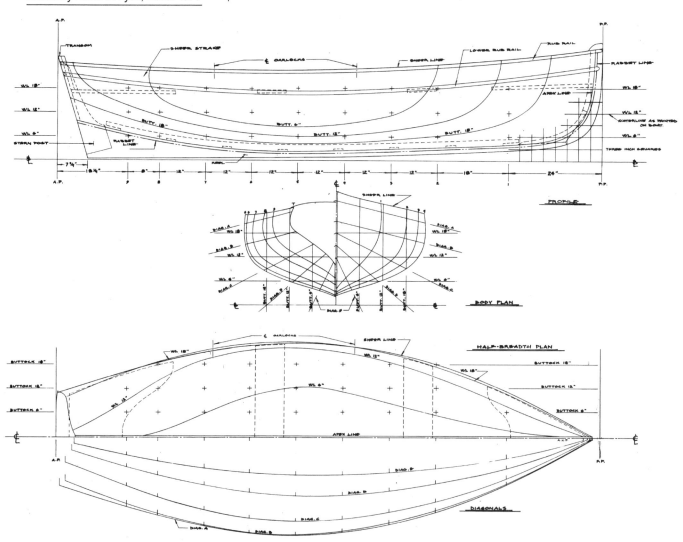

Capt. Hook
Pulling Boat from Southport, Maine

11' 11" x 3' 10"   ca. 1920

Accession No. 1974.472
Catalog No. 7.102

Drawn by Robert A. Pittaway, January 1976;
offsets and stem construction updated by
William D. Welte, March 1999

Maine builders called boats like this simply round-bottom rowboats, and they turned them out by the hundreds to meet the demands of the rusticators who began to flock to Maine about 1900. Whatever they're called, these boats are built exactly like the Whitehalls of Boston and New York. In shape they are similar as well, with a good bit of deadrise amidships, but they have more rake in the stem, letting them lift a bit more in waves, and the forefoot is slightly cut away for better maneuverability *Capt. Hook* was found in Southport, Maine. For years she served as a livery boat at Mystic Seaport's boat livery, where she was a favorite for a rower and a passenger or two. Quarter benches would let you take three passengers, even though it would be a bit of a load. A typical Whitehall in construction, she has prebent frames fastened to long, stout floor timbers. A hog piece supports the back rabbet over the deadwood, as does a long stem knee up forward. She is now retired from livery service, replaced by a Museum-built replica. An updated set of offsets was created from that lofting.

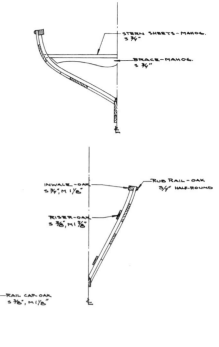

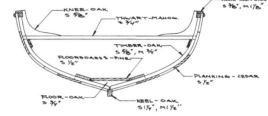

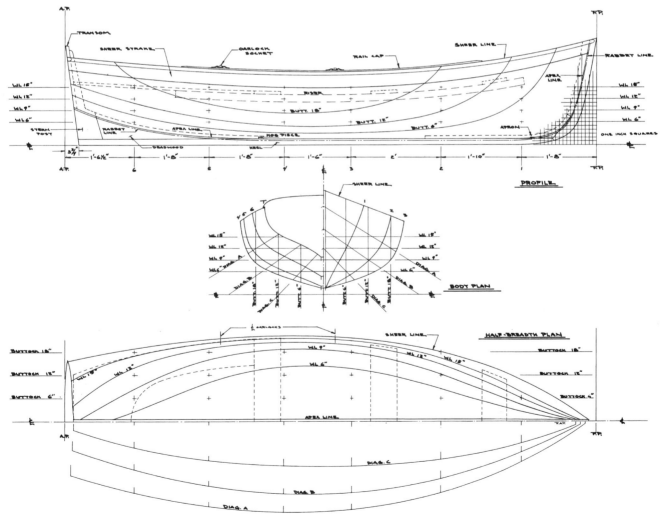

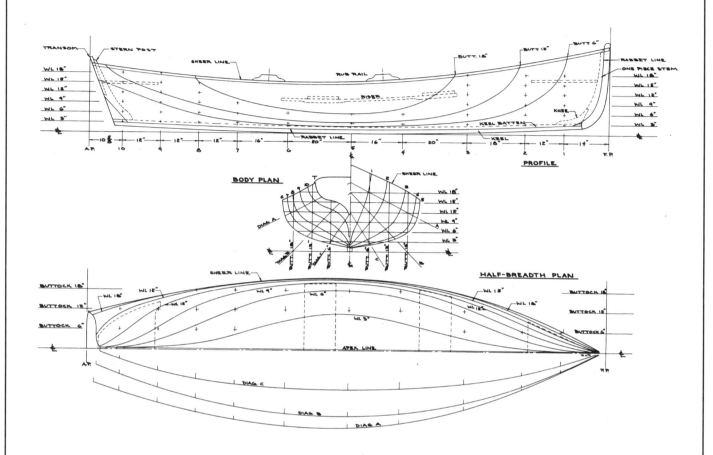

Whitehall-Style Boat, Probably for Livery Use

13' 7" x 3' 8"

Accession No. 1973.728
Catalog No. 7.118

Drawn by Robert A. Pittaway,
February-March 1974

This lapstrake Whitehall-style pulling boat demonstrates several short cuts that made her quick to build, including her garboard, keel, keel-batten construction, and her full-width, bent flat frames. With the demands from boat liveries and from yachtsmen needing tenders, boatbuilders developed these faster ways to build around 1900.

However, construction shortcuts are not evidenced in the elegant shape of this boat. She is narrower and much lighter (135 pounds) than the slightly shorter Boston Whitehall on the next page. She has a nice, highly tucked transom and a bit of rake in the stem. Like most of these shorter boats, she is set to pull with one, who could carry one or two passengers.

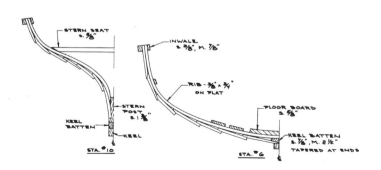

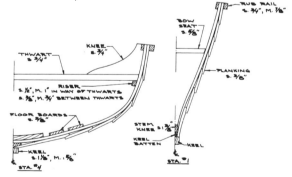

Boston Whitehall

13′ 2″ x 4′ 0″ ca. 1900-20

Accession No. 1969.584
Catalog No. 7.78

Lines taken off by John Gardner, 1969; drawn by Robert A. Pittaway, November 1973

John Gardner first saw this Whitehall in the 1940s when Charles Lawton, a veteran Whitehall builder, pointed her out while they were working together in Marblehead. Lawton said she was absolutely typical of a Boston Whitehall, although she was probably built in Maine. She is small for a working Whitehall, but is a true Whitehall in construction: her frames are square to the keel and beveled at the planking; the frames are deeper at the heel than at the head; the floor timbers cross the keel and connect the frames. In some Whitehalls like this one, the frame ends aft are boxed into the hog piece and there are no floors. Unusual is her one-piece stem, which has a 1/4″ of extra siding inside the planking to better support the planks. A boxed-in inwale and oak sheerstrake that projected beyond the planking provided the kind of strength needed if bouncing off a ship. This boat is not light—she totaled 213 pounds when we weighed her—but weight is to be expected with 1/2″ planking. Created as part of a serious study of Whitehalls, Rob Pittaway's construction plan is exceptionally detailed.

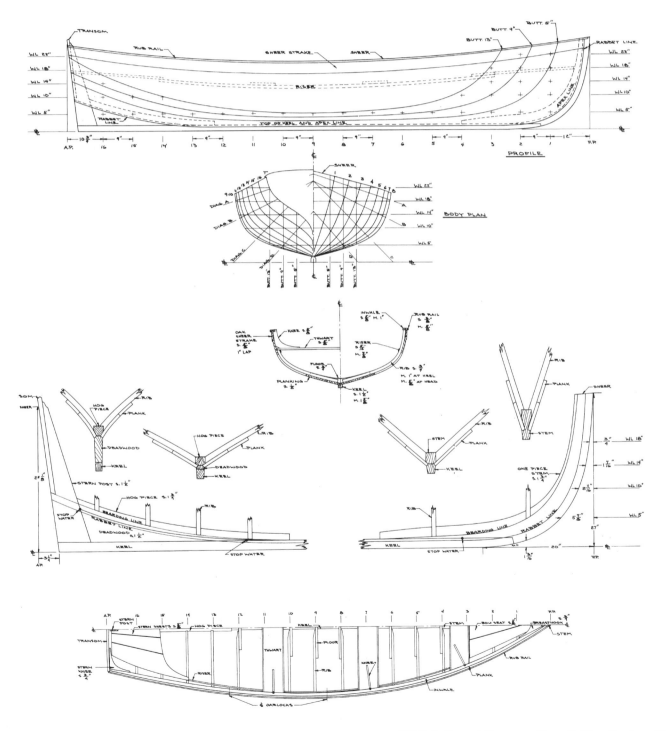

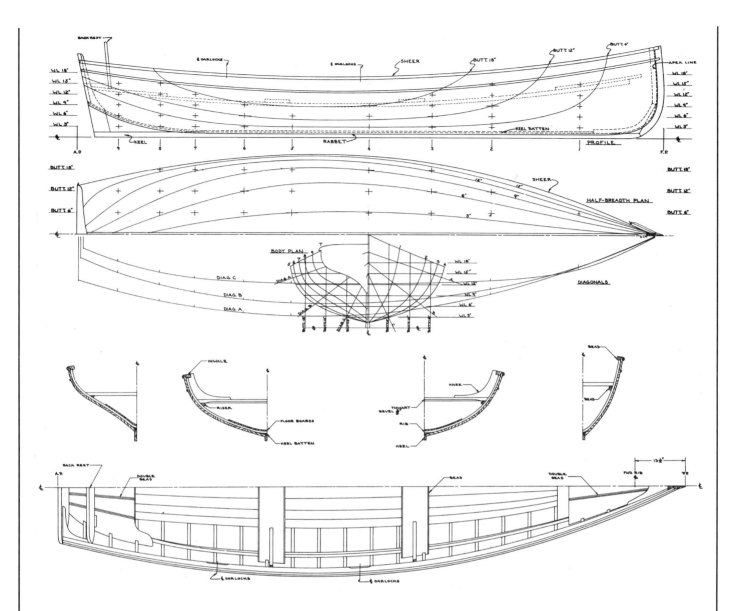

Whitehall-Type Pulling Boat by H.V. Partelow

14' 0" x 3' 10" ca. 1890

Accession No. 1973.39
Catalog No. 7.96

Drawn by Robert A. Pittaway, February 1973

This boat was produced by the Boston Whitehall-builder H.V. Partelow, for whom John Gardner's friend Charles Lawton worked as a young man. She is slimmer than most Whitehalls of this length. She has a keel batten and 22 steam-bent frames, bent over molds, a method developed about 1880, according to Lawton. This became the usual build-

ing technique for yacht tenders and other high-volume pulling boats.

This boat came to Mystic Seaport as a relic, missing the sternsheets and bow structure, which Rob Pittaway reconstructed for the plans. Plans include a detailed keel layout and plank layouts. Materials are not specified on the plan, but she was likely framed in oak and planked with cedar. Parts dimensions need to be scaled off the plan as only some are written out. Check the written dimensions; there are some minor errors in them, although they scale correctly. She is a good bit lighter than the Boston Whitehall (1969.584), scaling at 121 pounds without floorboards, sternsheets, and bow bracing. At 7/16", her planking is about as light as you can go and still caulk. She'd be a fun, fast boat for a

single rower. Rowed single with a fixed seat, slim boats in the 14'-16' range are quick. Still, she's large enough for two to row her with a passenger on board.

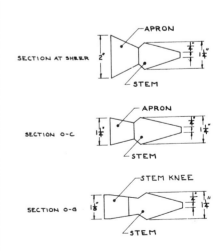

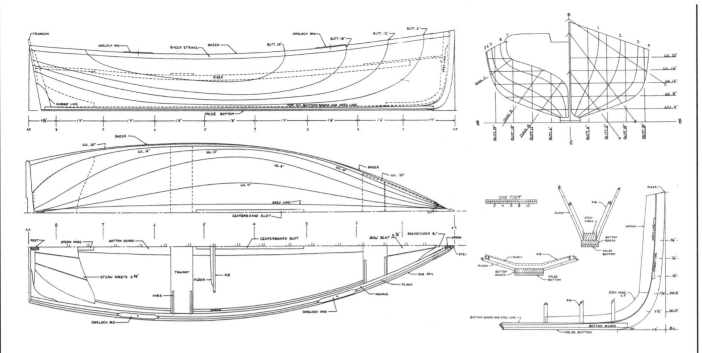

Temporary Moosabec Reach Boat

14′ 3″ x 4′ 2″ ca. 1900

Accession No. 1994.17
Catalog No. 17.21

Drawn by G. Anderson Chase, March 1974;
rig designed, January 1978

Bottom-board boats like reach boats, salmon wherries, Sea Bright skiffs, Seaford skiffs, and Adirondack guide-boats have a keel that is a wide plank. If you widened the plank you'd get a Piscataqua wherry, and if you added some planks alongside it you would get a dory. Their sterns are "built down" rather than having deadwood and a rabbet like the Whitehall types.

This Moosabec Reach boat came from the area of Castine, Maine, sometime before 1920, and probably dates to before 1900. Her owner, Andy Chase, brought her down to Mystic Seaport in March 1974, when he was in high school, and John Gardner helped him measure, draw, and repair the boat. Andy later designed a cat-ketch sailing rig. She has more freeboard than similarly sized Whitehalls, and her underwater shape is very different. Her bow and stern are longer and finer, and her

deadrise is carried out further, with a harder turn of the bilge. She has more flare up high forward. After sailing and rowing her for years, Andy donated her to the Museum, reporting, "She carries a tremendous load, rows and sails like a dream, is very fast, and is practically unsinkable." She is stable enough so that Andy could stand on her gunwale. That's not a bad evaluation from an owner who is now one of the Maine Maritime Academy's most experienced teachers and seafarers.

Construction is straightforward except for the challenge of the wicked hollow in the after garboard. John Gardner figured that a builder would need a bit of experience to reproduce her, but he noted hopefully, "surely we have not become so effete that there are not craftsmen among us today equal to the task." His full write-up is in Chapter 3 of his *Wooden Boats to Build and Use.* Andy Chase will build another Moosabec Reach boat someday, and he suggests that others build this design as well.

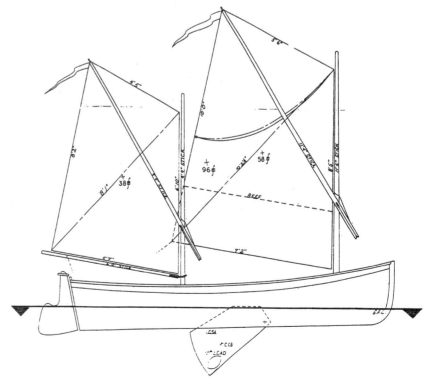

Whitehall, Mystic Seaport-Built

14' 9" x 4' 2"

Accession No. 1974.94
Catalog No. 7.80

Drawn by Robert A. Pittaway,
August-September 1973

The Maine Maritime Museum collection includes a bent-frame-style Whitehall built by the Rice Brothers of East Boothbay, Maine. It was measured to build this boat. But when drawing up the plans, Rob Pittaway and John Gardner changed the construction to classic Whitehall. The plans are especially complete, with backbone details; a transom expansion; and beads on the seat riser, sheerstrake, and thwart drawn full-size. Despite 9/16" planking she is only 40 pounds heavier than the Boston Whitehall (1969.584). Like most Whitehalls, this boat has elegant, long-

toed seat knees, a handsome and practical element that seems to be neglected in many of today's building projects. She is still in service in Mystic Seaport's boat livery. She rows well with

two, but she needs a passenger or some stern weight to keep her from griping in a crosswind. However, a longer boat of this model would suit a pair of rowers interested in speed.

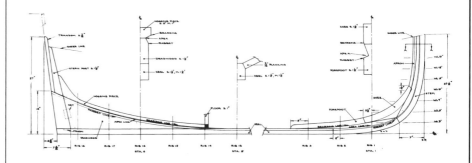

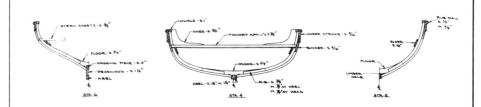

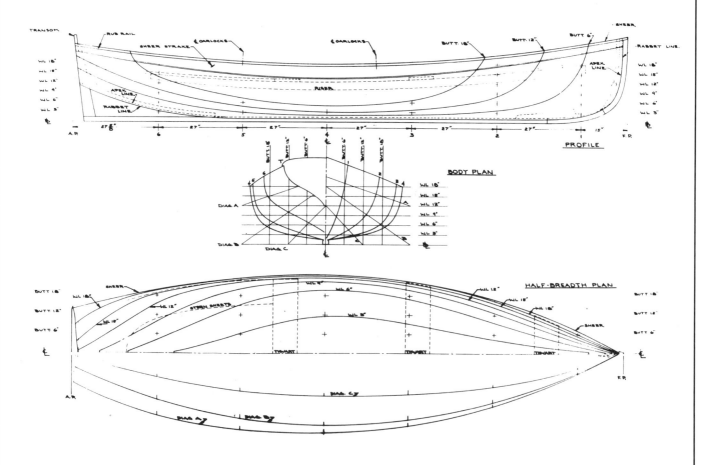

Whitehall by Sheldon

15′ 0″ x 4′ 1″   ca. 1900

Accession No. 1980.5
Catalog No. 7.111

Lines taken off March 1974; drawn by
Robert A. Pittaway, April 1974

Some six years before Townsend Horner donated her to Mystic Seaport, Rob Pittaway and the boat shop crew went over to Duxbury, Massachusetts, to measure this Whitehall. She came out of the shops of the Sheldon Company of Sheldonville, Massachusetts, which had shifted from producing mostly ship's boats to building for the recreational trade about 1890. This handsome, plainly finished Whitehall would have been at home in a boat livery. She is a little narrower and longer on the waterline than the Rice-based boat (1974.79, page 46), has a hollower stern and more deadrise, and is 2″ deeper. She's probably a touch faster through the water, especially being lighter with planking a scant 1/2″. Her forward rowing station is relatively further aft than the one in the Rice boat, and she'll likely handle better with just two people rowing. Her plans do not have the deadwood details of the Rice and Boston Whitehall (1969.584, page 43) plans, and the floorboards, plank widths, and stretcher locations were left out.

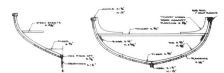

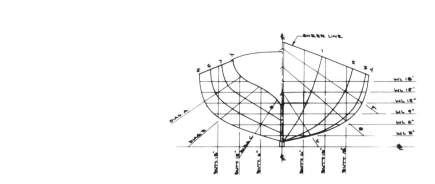

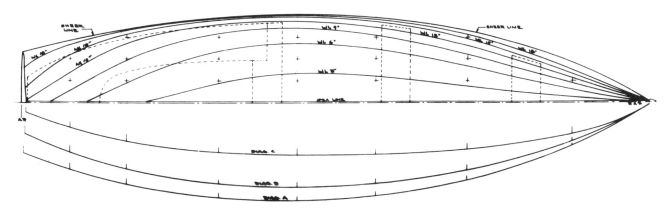

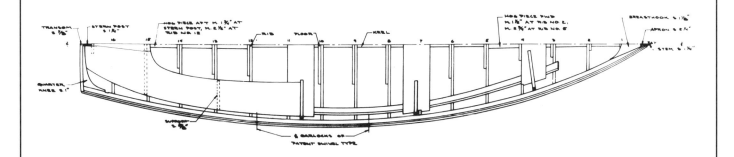

Winona
Pulling Boat by Bartlett

15′ 9″ x 4′ 1″ ca. 1911

Accession No. 1979.70
Catalog No. 7.113

Lines taken off by Robert Grover, June 1982;
drawn by William E. Mills, June 1983

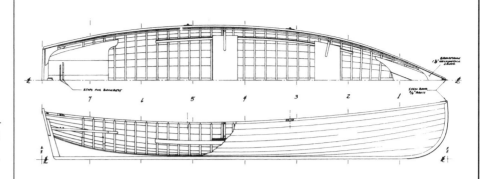

For a light, fast pulling boat in the Whitehall style, it would be hard to beat *Winona*. Built up at Lake George, New York, by Jared Bartlett, she was a standard boat furnished to liveries and summer folk alike. She has the plumb stem and straight keel of a Whitehall, but her stern does not have the characteristic hollow. Her sections approach a semicircle, giving less stability but also meaning lower wetted surface. But her lapstrake construction, with only 1/4" cedar planks and full steam-bent frames, is a simpler technique than the usual carvel Whitehall construction and yields a boat that is probably 100-150 pounds or more lighter than a similar Whitehall.

Winona's plans are the result of a combined effort, with Mystic Seaport volunteer Bob Grover measuring the boat and Bill Mills doing the fairing, the details, and the drawing. As she is set up, one rower could drive her to hull speed eas-

ily, making good use of the spoon oars that came with the boat. If two wanted to row, a passenger would be needed to have her track well. She is well set up for a couple, and this boat was used for moonlight rows and Sunday morning

trips to church, a pretty common way for young folks to dodge watchful parents. Her light construction calls for floorboards (missing from the boat) to protect the frames and plank edges from wear.

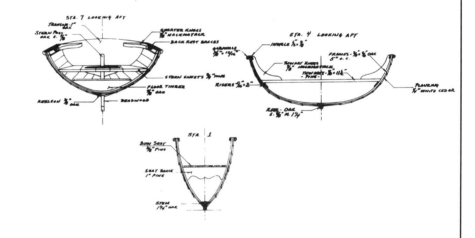

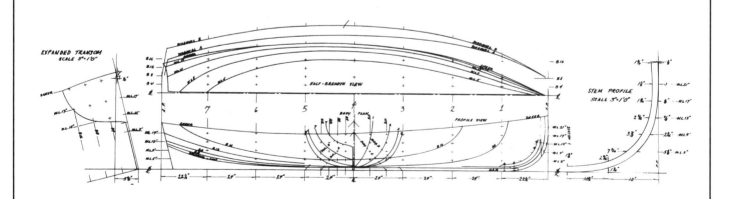

Bailey Whitehall

16′ 9″ x 3′ 7″ 1879

Accession No. 1954.211
Catalog No. 7.21

Drawn by Robert A. Pittaway,
December 1974-January 1975

Long and narrow, the Bailey Whitehall came out of one of Boston's fancy Whitehall shops about 1879. Her builder is unknown, but she was owned by the Bailey family, father and son, for 81 years. When she was built, sliding-seat rowing had been just introduced into the racing world, and this boat was set up with a slide. Her spoon oars and a set of wonderful pinned, yet feathering, oarlocks complement her style. You'll need some cross-handed skill to manage the oars as they run 8′ on a beam of 3′ 7″.

She has a pair of mast steps with metal bracing and a metal daggerboard trunk, but no rig details other than for the mast, which has two sheaves. Judging from the mast steps she could be sailed as a sloop or a cat, but there is no evidence of cleats or other details to indicate that she spent much time under sail. Her missing bronze daggerboard was thin enough to allow the slot to be cut through the 1″ keel.

She is built about as lightly as it is possible for a carvel boat with 3/8″ planks. The seat posts are turned; and all the floorboards, the seat riser, and the sheerstrake are beaded. Frames are inlet so the backbone can be stiffened by a full-length keel batten. While the plans do not show materials, her seats, interior structure, and sheerstrake appear to be mahogany. Even with the various metal pieces she weighs 313 pounds, which seems heavy unless she is mahogany planked as well. That is a bit over the contemporary boat-club rule that called for a minimum weight of 265 pounds. A few replicas of this boat have been built, but to my knowledge no one has attempted the metalwork yet.

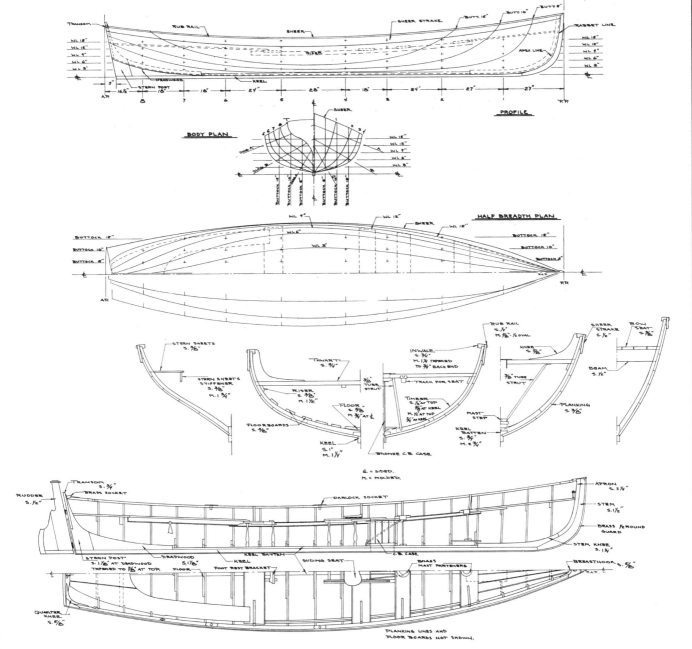

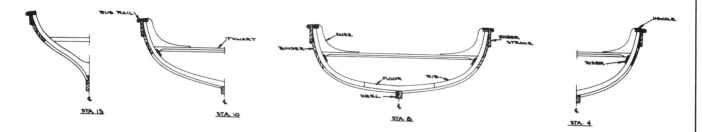

Sullivan Whitehall Model

20′ 0″ x 5′ 0″   ca. 1860

Accession No. 1975.435
Catalog No. 7.102

Drawn by William D. Welte, October 1997

This plan is taken from a 5′ builder's model in the Mystic Seaport collection, which hung in Dick Sullivan's boat shop on Atlantic Avenue in Boston. "Dick Sullivan's model was for a rowing boat to be used in races and was long and lean and straighter in the sheer than the boats used for business," Captain Charlton Smith wrote to W.P. Stephens. This model is the same one measured as part of the Historic American Merchant Marine Survey in the 1930s and called the Winde Whitehall, as the model then was owned by the Henry J. Winde Company in Charlestown. The model may date to the 1860s.

The model shows the boat with the interior completely installed and the sheer and binder and next planks hung, so that the boat was structurally stable enough to turn upside down for final planking. This was the usual method of Whitehall building. Built to a scale of 1/4" to the foot, the model's scantlings might be a touch heavy. Four seats cross the boat, which would allow her to be rowed as a four with coxswain, but the space in the stern would be tight. Three rowers would be better, but two would be a little scant for the best speed. Her beam is wide enough so that a pair of rowers might have used 9′ 6″ sweeps rather than sculls, or she might work well randan style, with a sculler amidships and sweep rowers forward and aft. With 3/4" planking, as drawn, the boat would not be light. To my knowledge, a replica of this boat has never been built, though the model certainly deserves replication.

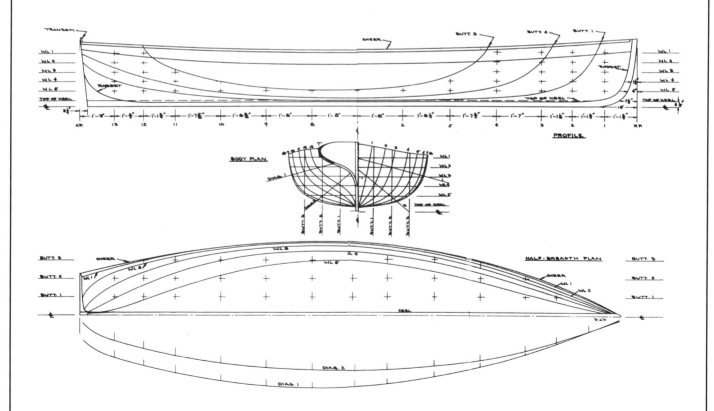

The Adirondack Museum at Blue Mountain Lake, New York, houses the world's largest collection of Adirondack guideboats. All of the boats offered here are in that collection, as is the Grant-built 16′ x 3′ 6″ *Virginia* (57.229.1), which was documented meticulously by John Gardner in Kenneth and Helen Durant's *The Adirondack Guide-Boat*.

Speed and light weight drove the evolution of the guideboat type as summer camps and resorts brought recreational fishermen, hunters, and rusticators to the Adirondack Mountains in the decades after the Civil War. Results in open-water racing indicate that guideboats are the fastest North American single-rower fixed-seat pulling boats. More interesting, they can handle far worse seas than the Adirondack lakes routinely produce. Still, they need careful handling. They use pinned, non-feathering oars, with considerable overlap. To their surprise, rowers accustomed to feathering their oars in the rough open ocean have found that this overlapping, non-feathering arrangement can be used in rough water, even though the boats were intended for more sheltered water use.

Ghost
Adirondack
Guideboat
by H.D. Grant

16′ 2″ x 3′ 2″

Catalog No. Misc 31 (Adirondack Museum 71.141.1)

Measured and drawn for the Adirondack Museum by David W. Dillion, 1984

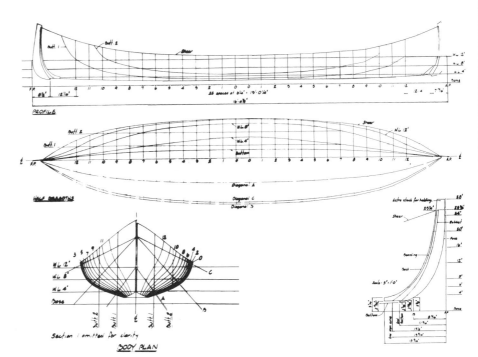

Guideboat
by Warren Cole

15′ 7″ x 3′ 6″

Catalog No. Misc 30 (Adirondack Museum 57.192.2)

Measured and drawn for the Adirondack Museum by David W. Dillion, 1984

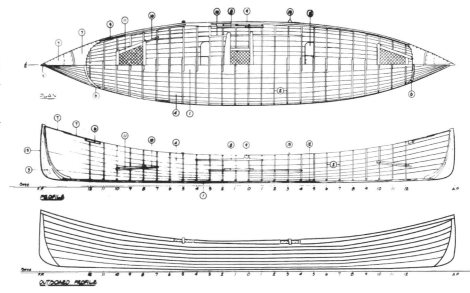

Guideboats are bottom-board boats with natural knees used as frames: the dory-building technique taken to the extreme. Builders developed a smooth-skin lap strake construction method now known as the guideboat lap. Lightness was achieved with meticulous attention to detail, such as planking that might have a 1/4" garboard, then the number one plank thinning from 1/4" at the lower edge to 3/16" at the upper. Stem profiles and construction details vary from builder to builder, with most preferring ends with a reverse curve, which trimmed weight. Deadrise varies from boat to boat. The small boats—like the 13' Parsons boat at 57 pounds and the 13' 6" Blanchard boat at 53 pounds—were best suited to be carried in to fish small ponds, for which they were called "raiders." The 16' guideboats are considered the best compromise between speed and carrying capacity, working well solo or carrying a guide and sport with their load of camping gear. The 16' *Ghost* weighs just 64 pounds, while the 15' 7" Cole boat weighs 59. Well-organized, experienced builders with patterns in hand could construct one in 200 to 250 hours. Like John Gardner's study of *Virginia*, the plans drawn by Dave Dillion do not require lofting; full dimensions are provided for each frame. Hallie Bond's *Boats and Boating in the Adirondacks* provides more historical information.

Today, guideboats are successfully built as frameless strip-planked boats and as semi-strip-planked boats with glued joints over laminated frames.

Guideboat by B. & I. Parsons

13' x 3' 2"

Catalog No. Misc 33 (Adirondack Museum 64.170.1)

Measured and drawn for the Adirondack Museum by David W. Dillion, 1984

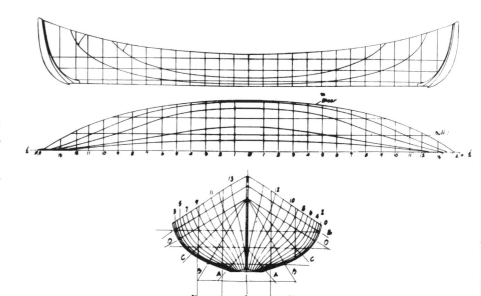

Guideboat by John Blanchard

13' 6" x 3' 2"

**Catalog No. Misc 17
(Adirondack Museum 57.122.1)**

Measured and drawn by Edson I. Schock, 1965; lofted and redrawn by Robert A. Pittaway, March 1975

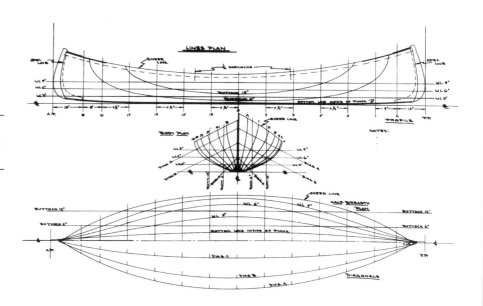

Like the Adirondacks, the St. Lawrence River's Thousand Islands area became popular with vacationers in the years after the Civil War. Residents refined the local pleasure and fishing skiff to take advantage of this new market for recreational boats. With local variations, by the 1890s they had standardized a long, slim, double-ended boat. Hulls were often asymmetrical, with the stern finer than the bow. When rowed solo, they rowed stern first. Lengths ran from 15' to 20'. Keels were wide oak planks rabbeted to take the garboards; steam-bent frames on 5"-6" centers supported cedar planking that could be guideboat-lapped or lapstrake. Full-length floorboards covered planks and frames, generally running all the way up to the seat risers. Gunwales were finished with in- and outwales, and long decks filled the boat's ends. A covering board covered the joint in the decks, and a shallow coaming around the cockpit tied everything together. The fanciest skiffs had nickel-plated hardware. Skiffs were generally set up for rowing with one and a passenger or two, or for solo rowing. Like guideboats, the skiffs usually had pins rather than oarlocks so the oars could be trailed while fishing. Oars were squared for balance inboard of the pin, which ran thorough the loom (and of course prevent feathering). Spritsail sailing rigs and folding centerboards could be found in the 20' skiffs, and some specialized 24' sailing skiffs with enormous rigs were built for intertown racing. The design moved out of the Thousand Islands area, and some builders outside the St. Lawrence River area produced them, including Sheldon in Boston. *The Rudder*, based in Watertown, New York, provided plenty of publicity for the type when it began publication in 1890.

The largest collection of St. Lawrence River skiffs is at the Antique Boat Museum in Clayton, New York. Its director, John Summers, has built one and has written the best brief history of the type to date: "'Probably the Most Beautiful Rowboat Afloat': The Form and Meaning of the St. Lawrence Skiff," *Material History Review 48*, Fall 1998. Andrew B. Steever and his wife Elizabeth measured four of the five boats listed here. An engineer, he devised a highly accurate jig to measure these boats to the outside of their planking. Andy drew them up and gave the plans to Mystic Seaport and the Antique Boat Museum. St. Lawrence skiffs have been built recently as strip-built and glued-lapstrake boats.

Annie
Skiff by A. Bain

17' 9" x 3' 3"   ca. 1885

Accession No. 1980.76
Catalog No. 7.116

Drawn by Andrew B. Steever, 1977

Annie came to Mystic Seaport's collection in 1980. Built by Bain at Clayton, New York, she is a fancy fishing skiff, with seats inlaid with cedar and butternut, butternut coamings, and birds-eye maple covering boards. At 140 pounds, she is lighter than most similar-sized skiffs, and has a little less deadrise than some.

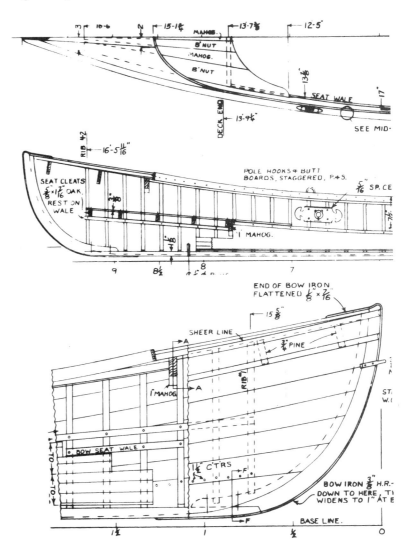

Clotilde
Skiff by Fitz Hunt

18′ 1″ x 3′ 7″ 1890
Catalog No. Misc. 14

Drawn by Andrew B. Steever, 1975

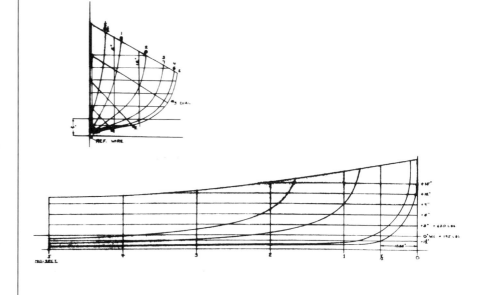

Of the skiffs listed here, the 195-pound *Clotilde* was one of the fanciest on the river, sporting a wide variety of woods in her trim. She was built by Fitz Hunt of Alexandria Bay, New York. With a symmetrical hull and guideboat-lap construction, she was known locally as one of the easier rowing models.

Skiff by A. Bain

18′ 2″ x 3′ 6″ 1885
Catalog No. Misc. 6

Drawn by Andrew B. Steever, 1973

The 201-pound Bain skiff is set up as a double and was raced regularly. She is now in the Antique Boat Museum collection.

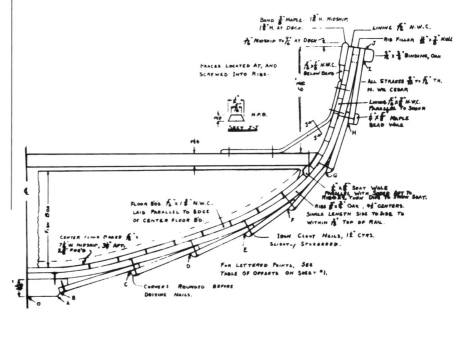

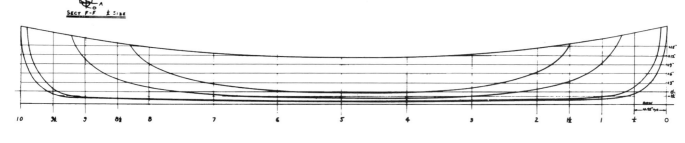

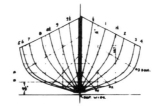

Bobby
Skiff by J.D. Hunt

20′ 5″ x 3′ 6″ pre-1905

Catalog No. Misc. 7

Drawn by Andrew B. Steever, 1974

J. Damar Hunt of Alexandria Bay, builder of *Bobby*, was known for fast skiffs. With her symmetrical shape and smooth, guideboat-lap planking, this 230-pound skiff is relatively sharp-ended and long, with more than the usual amount of deadrise and low ends to cut windage. She is set up with a single rowing station, but would make a nice double if the seating was worked out.

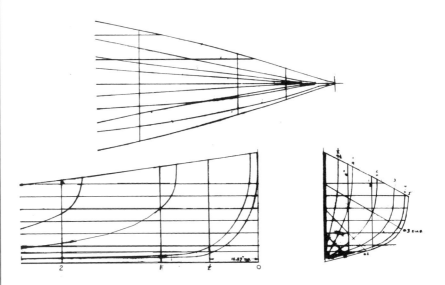

Skiff by
O. Sheldon & Co.

14′ x 3′ 2″ ca. 1900

Accession No. 1975.177
Catalog No. 7.88

Drawn by Ned B. Costello,
July 1977

Built in Massachusetts, far from the St. Lawrence, the skiff by Sheldon is lapstrake, with a hull that is marginally finer in the stern than the bow, which may be due to old age. Her rowing setup has a seat forward for rowing with a passenger and an after seat for solo rowing.

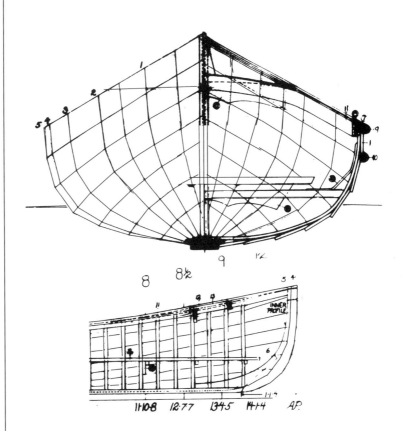

Rangeley Lake Boat by C.W. Barrett

14′ 7″ x 3′ 3″ ca. 1915

Accession No. 1974.1007
Catalog No. 7.45

Lines taken off by Robert A. Pittaway,
March 1973; revised by Edward F. McClave,
July 1978; construction drawing
by Edward F. McClave, September 1978

In 1978, Barry Thomas and Ed McClave selected Mystic Seaport's small Rangeley Lake boat as a subject for reconstruction and study with the aim of learning more about series wooden-boat building. The project resulted in a new set of plans for this boat, considerable information about Rangeley boatbuilding methods, and 20 boats. Rangeley boats appear to have been patterned after an 1870s boat owned by a member of the Oquossoc Angling Club, which was established on these western Maine lakes in 1869. Rangeley boats generally were 17′ long, intended to be rowed by a guide with a couple of sports, like the St. Lawrence River skiffs.

This 14′ 7″ boat is better suited to a single or pair of anglers. A relatively low-deadrise bottom gives stability for cross-boat fly casting. Common on these boats were round seats that accommodate sitting sideways when casting. Larger boats had trays built into the seats to hold fly books and other gear.

At 120 pounds, she is considerably heavier than similar-sized guideboats. But this Rangeley boat has fine ends, comes up to speed with little effort, and can be kept at better than a walking pace for hours. The stern is slightly finer than the bow. The oak plank keel has a rabbet that disappears near the first and last stations, which is well detailed in the plans. She is planked in 5/16″ cedar. Spruce stems have natural curves; the width of the lower stems, the fine ends, and the straight keel keep the boat tracking straight. Ed and Barry worked out a compression stem-bending technique for the boats built at the

Museum, which Ed described in "Bending Stems at Mystic Seaport," *WoodenBoat* 33, March/April 1981. The first boat they built can be rowed at the Museum's boat livery, where she is a favorite among discerning rowers.

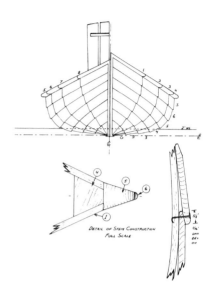

DETAIL OF STEM CONSTRUCTION
FULL SCALE

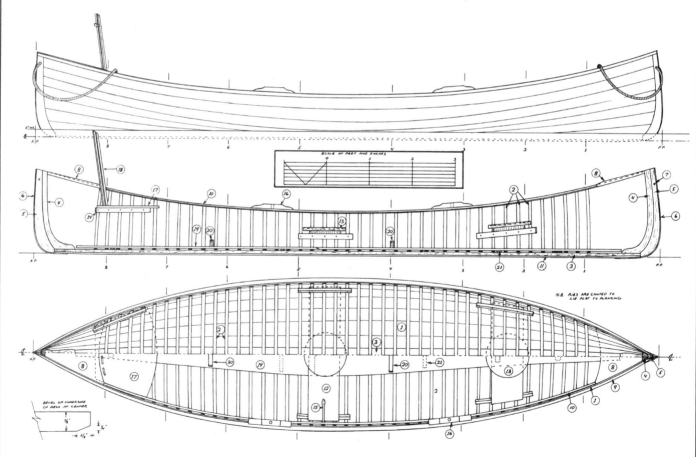

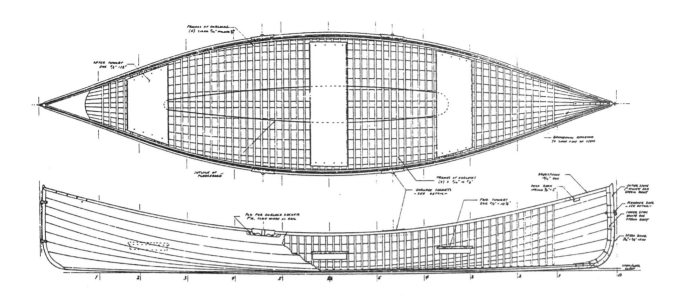

A.L.Rotch
Pulling boat by
Rushton, Model 109

14′ 3″ x 3′ 3″   ca. 1888

Accession No. 1960.261
Catalog No. 7.115

Drawn by William E. Mills,
January, June 1984

Rushton's light, sturdy pleasure rowboats were a mainstay of his shop from 1885 until the shop closed. The 109 model was built from 1885 to 1893, then probably "rebadged" and modified a bit to become one of the Iowa series in 1895. As Rushton described it in his catalog, "the Iowa was designed as a fast, easy-rowing, light-weight skiff. It is the boat you want for exercise, for running errands, and for pleasure." These boats may have been based on St. Lawrence River skiffs. However, they are lighter and simpler. The 109 has the flat bottom and hard bilge of the similar-sized Rangeley, but with 1/4" planking,

a lighter scantling keel, and lighter bent stems, it is in the 70-pound range. To keep things simple, Rushton built these as symmetrical boats. For longer ones, builders simply added some space amidships in the setup. As might be expected, on the water this boat handles much like the Barrett Rangeley.

The early boats could have simple solid breasthook/decks like this one. All of the post-1895 boats had strip-planked decks like the Vaux Jr. (Misc. 26, page 16). These boats took about 30-40 hours of work to assemble from pre-milled materials, using patterns for all planks and other parts. By adding Radix folding centerboards, Rushton could offer his rowing boats as lively rowing and sailing craft, a more successful combination in his longer and wider models.

Based on the success of the Rangeley boat project, the Model 109—which is about the same size but lighter and easier to build—became the next project at Mystic Seaport's boat shop. Ten of these boats were built using patterns based on this set of boat lines. Since then, Rushton's manuscript, "Knowledge," in the Adirondack Museum collection, has become better known (see Hallie Bond's article, "J. Henry Rushton's Books of Knowledge," *The Apprentice* 12, Autumn 1990). It lists dimensions for plank patterns for all models, which have been tested and found to work. Some commercial builders have continued to produce this model. The boat should build easily in glued lapstrake, although I do not know if that approach has been tried yet. Bill Mills's plans include drawings for the hardware.

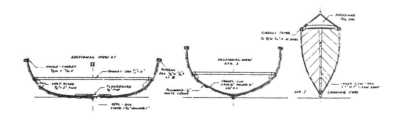

Peapod by Gardner

14′ 2″ x 4′ 5″   1971

Accession No. 1971.237
Catalog No. 7.42

Designed and drawn by John Gardner, 1971

John Gardner modeled this peapod shortly after coming to Mystic Seaport in 1971. She was designed for rowing ease, with a bit more deadrise and hollower ends than are found in many pods. John gave her a bit livelier sheer for looks. In creating her, he approached it as a fisherman might have, drawing some rough lines, carving a half model, then lofting the boat from the model. These plans were drawn from the lofted lines. Since she's a true double-ender like most peapods, the drawing shows a quarter of the boat, with the lines on top of each other as they came off the lofting table. John's account in *Building Classic Small Craft* describes her design and construction—1/2″ cedar planking on continuous frames (5/8″ molded by 7/8″ wide) spaced at 8″—but some other plans will need to be reviewed for details. She has enough deadrise to allow a keel batten to back up the narrow scantling keel.

The boat John's assistant Sylvester Costelloe then built is still in use in the Museum's boat livery. Like most peapods, she is deep and heavy, a little much perhaps for the Mystic River. But she is steadier than most delicate lake and river boats, and she is good for more open water and rougher service. The minimum size used in fishing was about 14′. Recently, smaller pods have been developed as tenders for recreational users.

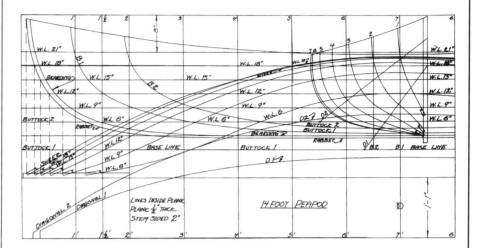

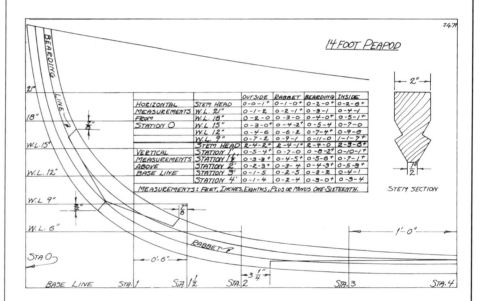

		OUTSIDE	RABBET	BEARDING	INSIDE
HORIZONTAL MEASUREMENTS FROM STATION 0	STEM HEAD	0-0-1+	0-1-0+	0-2-0+	0-2-8+
	W.L. 21″	0-1-2	0-2-1+	0-3-1	0-4-1
	W.L. 18″	0-2-0	0-3-0	0-4-0+	0-5-1+
	W.L. 15″	0-3-0+	0-4-2+	0-5-4	0-7-0
	W.L. 12″	0-4-6	0-6-2	0-7-4+	0-9-0
	W.L. 9″	0-7-2	0-9-1	0-11-0	1-1-7+
VERTICAL MEASUREMENTS ABOVE BASE LINE	STEM HEAD	2-4-2+	2-4-1+	2-4-0	2-3-8+
	STATION 1	0-5-4+	0-7-0	0-8-2+	0-10-1+
	STATION 1¼	0-3-3+	0-4-5+	0-5-6+	0-7-1+
	STATION 2′	0-2-3+	0-3-4	0-4-3+	0-5-3+
	STATION 3′	0-1-5	0-2-5	0-3-2	0-4-1
	STATION 4′	0-1-4	0-2-4	0-3-0+	0-3-4

MEASUREMENTS: FEET, INCHES, EIGHTHS, PLUS OR MINUS ONE-SIXTEENTH.

14 FOOT PEAPOD

STEM SECTION

Peapod from North Haven by Whitmore

14′ 3″ x 4′ 4″   ca. 1929

Accession No. 1985.135
Catalog No. 7.124

Lines taken off, 1984; drawn by
John Gardner, 1984

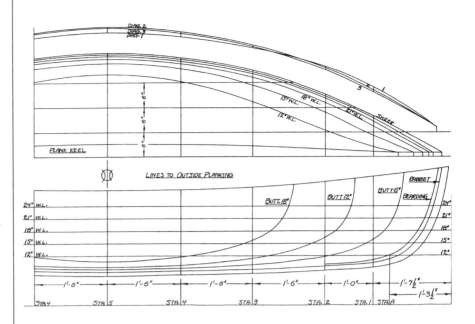

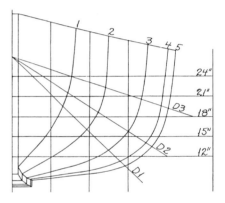

Alton Whitmore built this boat at North Haven, Maine, about 1929 for a local fisherman. She came into the hands of Captain Allison Ames of Camden, Maine, from whom John Gardner bought her in 1966. In 1985, after he and Bill Mills built a copy, John gave her to Mystic Seaport. His chapter in *Classic Small Craft You Can Build* describes the Whitmore building process, commonly used for both peapods and small transom-stern tenders on the Maine coast. It is like the old Whitehall method, where the sheerstrake, the binder, and the interior structure go in the boat before she is planked. The Whitmore pod is unusual in having secondary breasthooks that tie the seat risers together for extra strength. This boat has 1/2″ planking, except for a heavier sheerstrake. Her flat frames (5/8″ x 1 1/8″) butt at the keel and are spaced widely at 9″, with 2″ half timbers in between. Like most lobstering peapods, she has a heavy oak plank keel that needs to be steam-bent to take the required amount of rocker. Her layout is set up for fishing: she'd be bow-down without a load, stern-down when you reversed direction for standing up and push-rowing to work lightly among the rocks. She has an inch or so less sheer and a bit flatter deadrise than the peapod John Gardner modeled (1971.237, page 58). One owner reported, "she didn't blow about and held steadier in a wind than any boat he had ever used." At Mystic Seaport's boat livery you can test her.

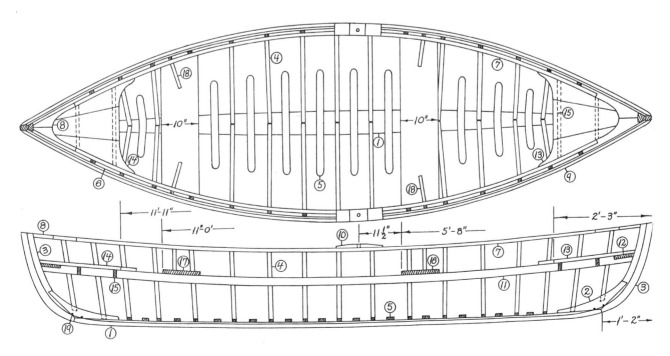

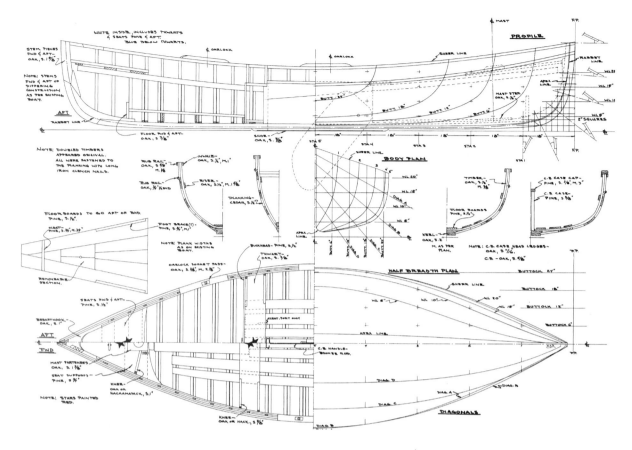

Red Star Sailing Peapod from Deer Isle by Nate Eaton

14' 11" x 4' 5"   ca. 1920

Accession No. 1970.638
Catalog No. 7.120

Drawn by Robert A. Pittaway, June 1976

Yet more variations on peapod design are represented by this one, built on Deer Isle, Maine, about 1920 to serve as a daysailer for her owner, and later as a yacht tender. At almost 15', she is set up nicely for two to row, but she'd be a bit bow-down with one rowing solo. Compared to the Whitmore pod (1985.135, page 59), her stems are straighter and she has fuller ends; her deadrise is similar to that of the Whitmore, but she has more sheer and is a deeper boat. She has a similar rabbeted oak plank keel, which makes it easy to put in a centerboard trunk. She has continuous timbers (sided 1/2",

molded 7/8") on 6" centers, with doubled frames that run across the boat from seat riser to seat riser. Planking is the common 1/2" cedar. In developing

the plans, Rob Pittaway drew a considerably larger spritsail than the small triangular sail that came with the boat.

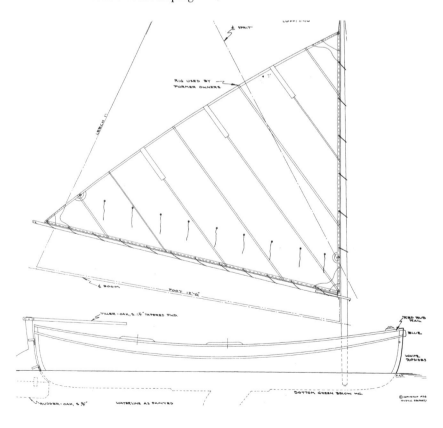

Peapod from Cape Split, Maine

16' 2" x 4' 2"   ca. 1880

Accession No. 1967.302
Catalog No. 7.109

Drawn by William E. Mills, May 1982

Stretching a peapod out to 16' gives a powerful, fast rowing boat. This boat, from Cape Split, Maine, was used as a lobstering pod for 50 years or more. It must have been tricky to balance her when hauling traps, as this boat has a shallow arc midsection that is more like a canoe or guideboat. She has only about 14" of depth amidships, and her stems are about 2' high, which is inches lower than those of the other pods in this catalog. Local fishermen called it the best "row-pod" on the coast, but "very titlish—wars'en canoe." The last owner told the donor that he once

slipped while hauling traps, landing on the rail amidships. She shipped about two buckets of water but stayed upright.

The boat was a wreck when the donor bought her for $25. After soaking her for a couple of weeks to get her tightened up, he found he could pull her at 6 knots with only 7' oars. With the boat empty, he could put two-thirds of his 185 pounds on the rail; with two 70-pound boys in the boat, he could sit on the rail. He never restored her; when he got her the keel had dropped a bit, taking the garboard with it, a shape that had been locked in by a repair.

She is planked a bit more lightly than most working pods, with 7/16" cedar, and her frames (7/16" x 3/4") are on 5" centers. Her stern is slightly sharper and lower than the bow. She is quite straight-keeled, with a square oak timber backed by a keel batten. She'd be a quick boat for two with the seats slightly rearranged to keep the bow in trim, or a fun boat for solo rowing or for carrying a single passenger.

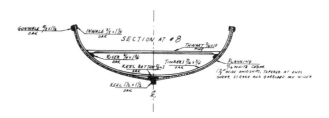

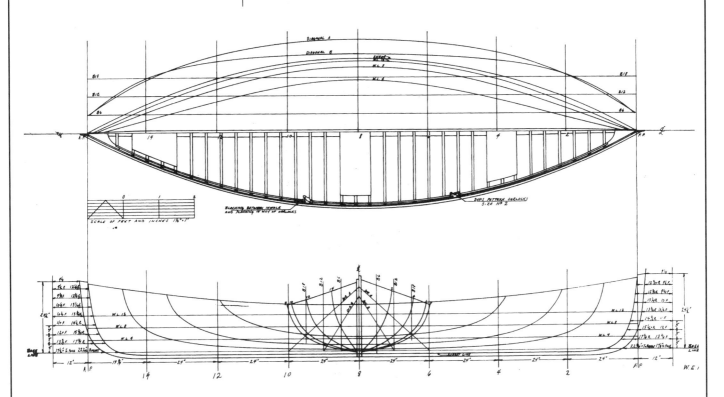

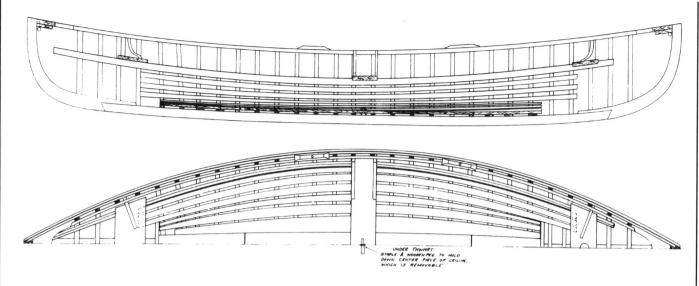

Peapod, Probably from Deer Isle, Maine

16′ 0″ x 4′ 5″   ca. 1900

Accession No. 1959.1472
Catalog No. 7.41

Drawn by Edson I. Schock, July 1963;
alterations May 1967

This 16′ peapod has a mast thwart and step for setting a small sail to help the user when the wind served. These pods sail surprisingly well without bene- fit of keel or rudder. Her planking is a bit heavy at 9/16″, with continuous flat frames (5/8″ x 1 1/8″ like the Whitmore pod) on 6″ centers. Near the boat's ends, there are some bent floor timbers, and the stern has a knee that helps hold things together.

The plans (below) show the boat's layout when she arrived at Mystic Seaport, with two extra thwarts to carry passen- gers and for a second rower. The plans (above) also show her as rebuilt with more floorboards and the removal of the seats that would have interfered with lobstering. The bottom is relatively flat, with a hard turn to the bilge. She is as deep and as high-ended as the smaller 14′ lobstering pods. Her keel is a rela- tively deep, narrow piece of oak with some rocker, which is handy for holding course under sail, but is different from other peapod keels. Her ends are full, with a stern sharper than the bow, which should aid tracking.

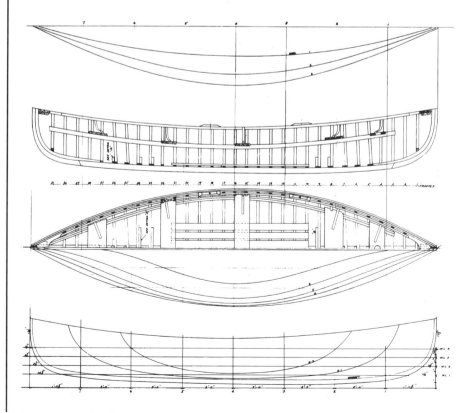

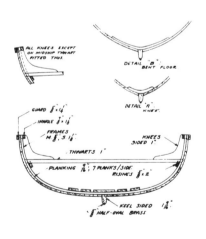

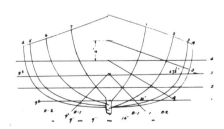

Delaware Ducker Rowing and Pushing Model

14' 10" x 3' 10"

Accession No. 1969.98
Catalog No. 7.103

Drawn by Robert A. Pittaway,
September 1976

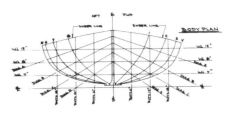

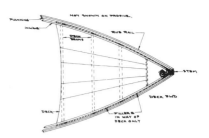

In comparison with the robust peapod of Maine, the Delaware ducker, or railbird boat, is a different kind of working double-ender. This one is a rowing and pushing model, designed to be propelled by pole and oar. Duckers were developed for negotiating the marshes of the lower Delaware River, poling through marsh grass on the tides and traveling narrow creeks. But they also had to be seaworthy enough to deal with the nasty chop that develops on open bays. These boats are set up with a pushing platform or deck in the stern. There is a removable seat aft, from which they could be push-rowed. Normal rowing was from a movable gunning box or seat amidships, which could be shifted aft for solo rowing. The gunning box is missing from this boat, as is the removable floor flat or floorboard.

These duckers are lightly built, with plank keels and lapstrake construction. This one is planked with 3/8" cedar, and the frames (left out on this plan) are 3/8" x 3/4" oak, laid on the flat, on 9" centers. Planking runs are pretty

straight. Originally the boats were built over three molds. More recently, glued-lapstrake construction has been used quite successfully for these boats. This boat has a nice bit of crown to her fore-deck, and her hull is slightly asymmetrical, with a bit of extra buoyancy aft to support the pusher. Compared with other rowing boats of this size and weight (something upwards of 100 pounds), she has a bit fuller ends, which helps out as the boat is pushed towards hull speed, and lifts the ends over the chop. A ducker will run easily

around 4 knots under oars, which is a bit faster than a similar-sized Rangeley boat. In an 1874 Philadelphia newspaper, I ran across a note from a veteran ducker oarsman challenging anyone in the United States to race their single, oarlocks-on-the-gunwale workboat against his ducker for stakes from $1,000 to $5,000. I never learned if anyone took up the challenge, but in the years before the final development of Adirondack guideboats and St. Lawrence skiffs, his supporters' money was probably pretty safe.

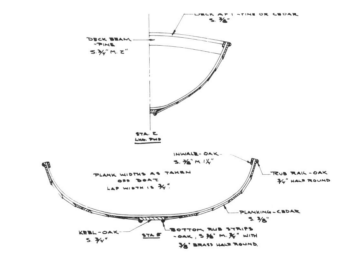

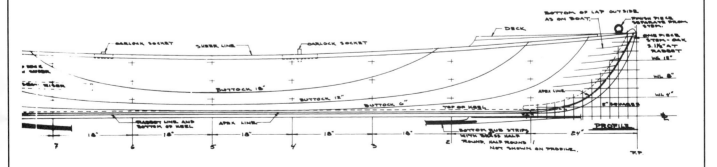

York Delaware Ducker, Sailing Model

15' 0" x 4' 0"

Accession No. 1969.821
Catalog No. 7.123

Lines taken and lofted by Peter Vermilya; drawn by David W. Dillion, March–May 1987

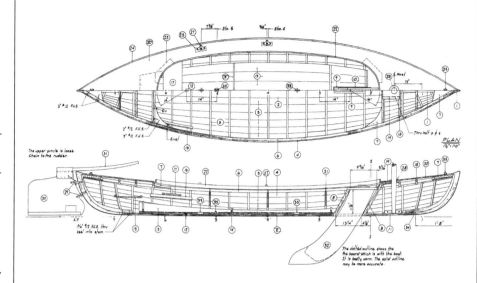

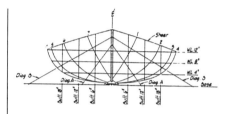

Called the York ducker after John B. York, the original owner, this ducker is one of the most complete Delaware duckers in existence. Dave Dillion's plans reflect this, recording the boat as well as the gunning box seat, the tent for camping, the awning for rowing on a summer's day, the removable shelf aft for lunch, the counterbalanced oars, and the spars, push poles, and hardware. After the Civil War, Philadelphia had plenty of sophisticated boatbuilders, as demonstrated by products like this and other duckers that are in collections at Mystic Seaport, Independence Seaport Museum at Philadelphia, and the Chesapeake Bay Maritime Museum at St. Michaels, Maryland. The York ducker represents the final evolution of the type from a simple gunning boat to a boat that, by virtue of decked ends, washboards, and a coaming, was able to go after ducks in winter, yet be used for leisurely summer sailing and camping trips.

The York ducker has an inch or two more sheer than some others that have been recorded—notably *Greenbrier*, a similar sailing model whose drawings are available from Independence Seaport Museum. She has relatively flat floors, much like the pushing ducker (1969.98, page 63), that give her a bit better stability, letting the boat be shallower amidships than *Greenbrier*. Sailing duckers run to about 150 pounds with floorboards, most of the additional 50 pounds coming from the deck. Built as glued-lap boats, their weight drops to about 100 pounds, and built in two-layer, cold-molded cedar they come in around 70 pounds. Then they become lively indeed.

Hiking sticks and straps are the main modern alterations seen on duckers, in addition to buoyancy bags if they're sailed regularly in heavy air. These boats are weight-sensitive; you want to be on the high side and keep your feet under you if it is gusty. Whatever their weight, they have enough fullness in the ends to plane under sail. The dagger-board is more efficient than a similar-sized centerboard as there is no slot drag; the boat has a filler block for the daggerboard slot when rowing. I'm a bit prejudiced as I own a *Greenbrier* reproduction, but I know of no other traditional design that is as versatile. It's a fine, lively sailing boat for one or two, and an outstanding rowing boat for one. Articles in *WoodenBoat* 48, September/October 1982, and 148, May/June 1999, provide more information about the type.

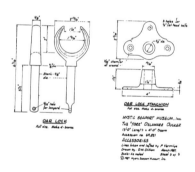

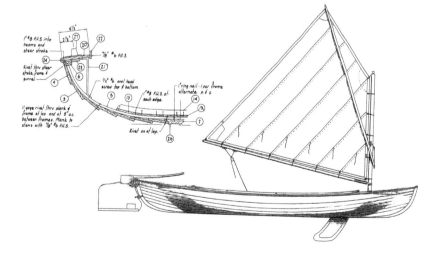

Most hunting boats are created for very specific purposes. Low profile "floats" were designed to be anchored in the midst of a flock of decoys, with the gunner lying prone. Scull floats could used to sneak up on a flock of ducks that might have been lured in by decoys, with the gunner sculling while lying down.

Brant
Duck Boat

10′ 3″ x 4′ 7″ 1894

Accession No. 1957.917
Catalog No. 7.25

Drawn by Edson I. Schock

Brant was used around the area of Groton, Connecticut, as a mobile blind that could be rowed into place. The wide wings and coaming helped keep waves out of the cockpit. If she was set out with a support boat, ballast could be added to *Brant* to lower her further into the water. She was nicely built with a bottom board and a highly V'd hull, with lots of rocker. Seaworthiness was not her strong point.

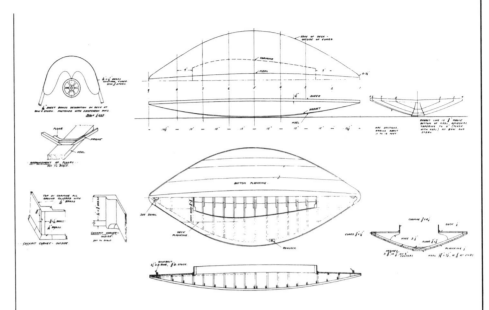

Connecticut River
Duck Boat

12′ 5″ x 3′ 5″

Accession No. 1959.208
Catalog No. 7.62

Drawn by Edson I. Schock

The Connecticut River duck boat came from around Essex. She can be sculled using a single oar through a port in the stern; she can be rowed; or she can be sailed, which is most unusual for duck boats. In hull shape, she is a nice flatiron, sharpie-style skiff. She needs little forward freeboard as she is fully decked.

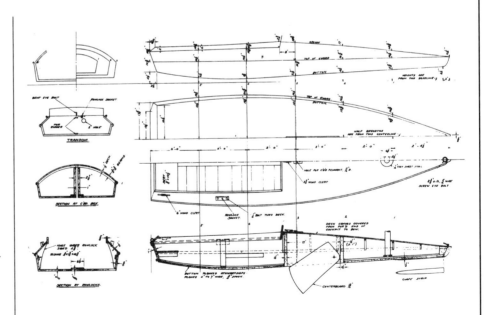

Great Bay, New Hampshire, Duck Boat

14′ 8″ x 3′ 4″

Accession No. 1961.559
Catalog No. 7.34

Drawn by Edson I. Schock

On New Hampshire's Great Bay and on Maine's Merrymeeting Bay, sculling duck boats were also common. This one from Great Bay is a highly sophisticated model. She is built like a sneakbox with a round bottom that curves up to a timber along the sheer that is called a harpin; the deck curves down to the same timber. Sawn ring frames and knees support the deck, and there are bent frames for the hull in between. She is lightly built with 5/16″ planking and decking covered with canvas. Most interestingly, she has a round stern and deck under which there is a tunnel that comes into the cockpit, which allows a sculling oar to be used without being seen from above. With her length, she would row well. Later duck-boat builders of Great Bay dropped the round stern and put on a transom at the rear of the cockpit for an outboard.

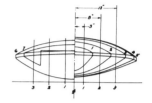

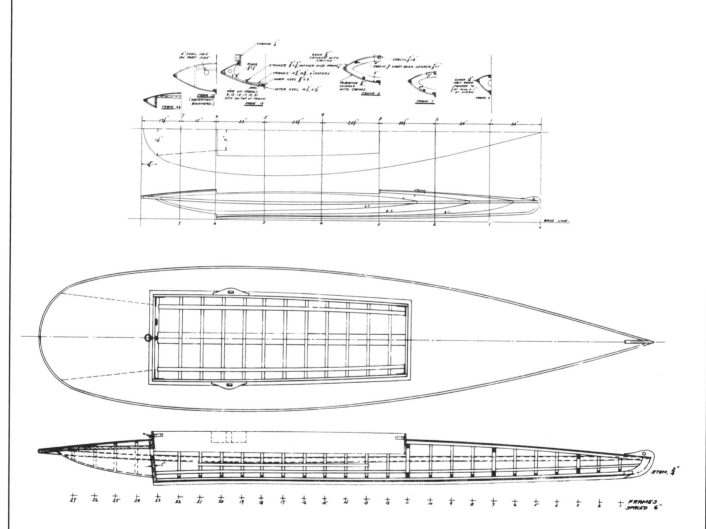

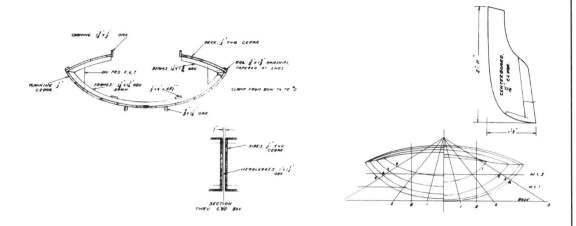

Barnegat Bay Sneakbox

12' 1" x 4' 2" ca. 1910

Accession No. 1961.915
Catalog No. 7.57

Drawn by Edson I. Schock

The Barnegat Bay sneakbox must be one of the most famous American small sailing craft. Nathaniel Bishop's 1879 book, *Four Months in a Sneakbox*, which details his trip down the Ohio and Mississippi and along the Gulf Coast, transformed them from a local gunning boat to a nationally known small boat type. Bishop paid $75 for his 200-pound *Centennial Republic* at a time when canoe-builders were getting $125 for a fully found Rob Roy.

This is one of the 12' gunning sneaks, like Bishop's, with a bottom and deck shaped basically like a spoon. The harpin just catches the planks in the bow. Planking and decking of this and all the gunning sneaks is 1/2" cedar, as is the keel, which is just a center plank. Frames in the old boxes were sawn cedar as well; this one, built about 1910 by Howard Perrine in Barnegat, New Jersey, has oak frames. The bottom curves of the sneakbox all come from one master curve, which eases construction. Today, laminated frames could replace the natural cedar crooks. Somewhat slow under oars, she'd still be a fun, safe boat for single-handed cruising, and still a functional and useful gunning boat.

Prospective builders would need to consult other sources to build this boat, as the plans do not include a sailing rig or oars. There is a full bibliography of sources in *Mystic Seaport Watercraft*.

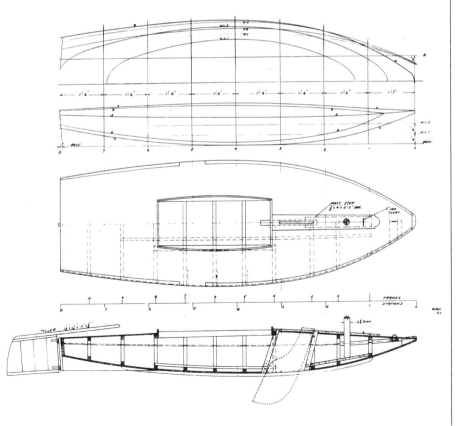

Melonseed

13' 10" x 4' 10"

Catalog No. Misc. 5

Measured by Wayne Yarnell and Barry
Thomas, 1974

More sophisticated, larger, and heavier (and more expensive) than the gunning sneakboxes were the melonseeds of Little Egg Harbor, New Jersey, and their cousins the Seaford skiffs of Great South Bay, Long Island. Judging from surviving information, the former were far more numerous than the latter. But the melonseed is now one of the best-known adaptations, as commercial builders have replicated the melonseed illustrated in Howard Chapelle's *American Small Sailing Craft*. Melonseeds and Seaford skiffs are somewhat drier than equivalent small sneakboxes and can carry more than one person. Rowing is not these boats' strength; the bays of New Jersey and Long Island are pretty open and have wind winter and summer, so they're designed to sail.

Barry Thomas built one of the small melonseeds for himself and his then-10-year-old son. He wrote eloquently about its performance in the 1974 *Log of Mystic Seaport*: "She starts to move, the river wavelet slapping her, then down she lays in a gust, lee bow wave roaring, deck under water in a rush. Don't crack the sheet, and don't let her come up! Just strap her down and she tears along."

When Barry had a chance to measure another melonseed with New Jersey boat historian Wayne Yarnell in 1974, he jumped at it. This one was found in Northfield, New Jersey. She is a bit bigger than the one Chapelle drew. She is lapstrake built of 1/2" cedar over 1" bent oak frames. She has more rake to the stem and more deadrise than the Chapelle boat. Her stern kicks up sharply, which may be why the plank keel is straight and has oak deadwood set on it with a rabbet to take the garboard. It seems to have been more com-

mon to spring or bend the oak keel up and attach a skeg. With the boat were two leg-of-mutton sails, one with a club.

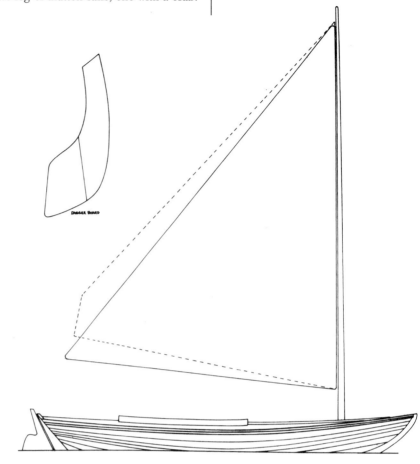

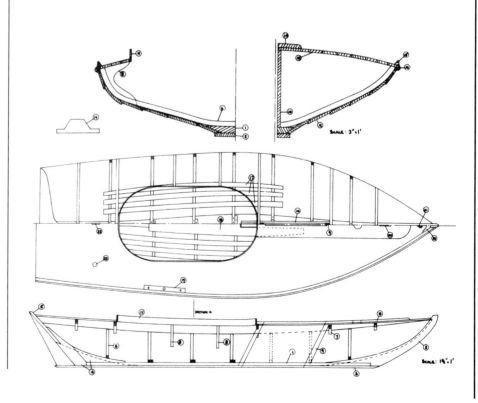

In 1996, Mystic Seaport's boat shop built a Seaford skiff to replace the Ketchum skiff that had been serving the Museum's boat livery for some years. The boatbuilders took the opportunity to research these boats a bit more and draw another one. The Verity from the Seaford Historical Society on Long Island caught their eye, and they drew her, but decided to build another Ketchum. You can now sail her replica at the Museum's boat livery. She is named for Helen Packer, the long-serving secretary who helped the boat shop and handled the sale of boat plans.

Besides similarities in general shape and decking, Seaford skiffs and melonseeds both have a long plank keel. Frames originally were sawn cedar roots. Keels aft are built two ways. Generally, but not always, melonseeds have a skeg with their flat plank keel bent up for the tuck. The Seaford skiff has a straight keel, with the garboards bent down to form a hollow box aft, similar to the construction of Maine's reach boats and salmon wherries, and New Jersey's Sea Bright skiffs. It's like the stern of a dory, with the first broad plank coming in at an acute angle. It appears that Seaford skiffs all had centerboards, whereas down in New Jersey the watermen favored daggerboards for small sneakboxes, melonseeds, and Delaware duckers.

Seaford Skiff by Charles Verity

14′ 2″ x 4′ 0″ 1910

Catalog No. Misc. 44 (Seaford Historical Society)

Lines taken off by Barry Thomas, Chris Rawlings, and Danny Olsen, January 1996; drawn by Chris Rawlings

When you look at the 1910 Verity skiff, you can see why Barry and Chris chose her to draw her. She has a touch more sheer than the Ketchum boat; otherwise her lines are quite close. But the Verity boat is older and has the sawn frames and floor timbers of the old-style hunting boats. She has 4″ less depth overall, and flatter floors. The plans do not show the sail plan that the shop developed, which was based on the Ketchum boat.

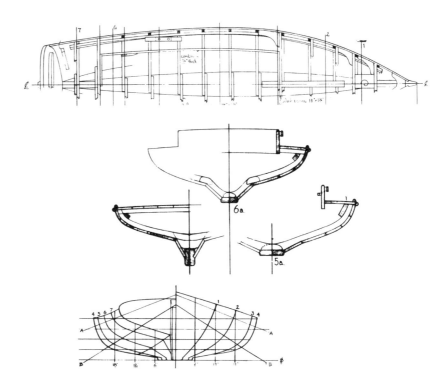

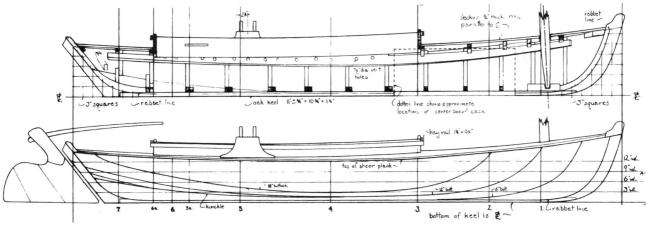

Brownie
Seaford Skiff
Attributed to
Charles Verity

12' 7" x 4' 2"   ca. 1883

Accession No. 1962.674
Catalog No. 7.58

Drawn by Edson I. Schock

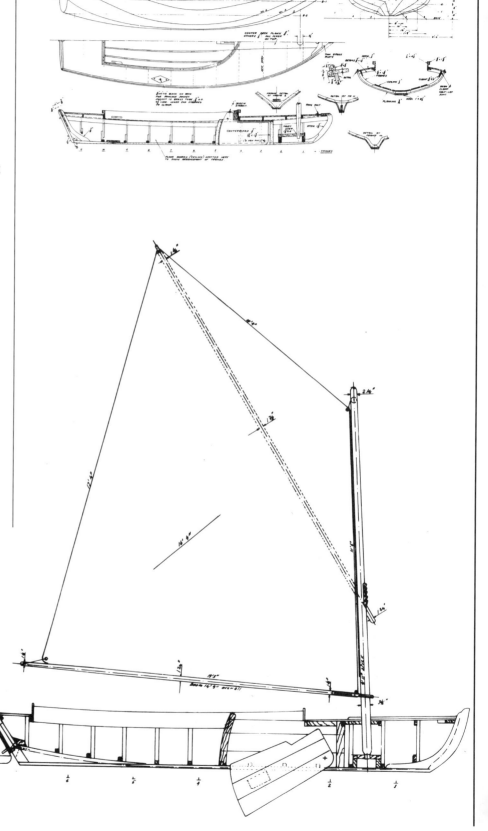

The plans of *Brownie* and *Ro Ro* are less detailed than those of the other boats. *Brownie* is a small gunning skiff best suited to single-handing like a sneakbox. She has a curved cockpit coaming and her maximum beam well ahead of amidships. Her 1" x 1" oak frames and floor timbers are doubled and staggered.

Ro Ro
Seaford Skiff

13' 6" x 4' 4"

Accession No. 1976.149
Catalog No. 7.100

Drawn by Dr. Peter Biancini

Ro Ro's keel structure is an exception: she has the Jersey melonseed bent keel. Only her framing and planking is dimensioned on the plans.

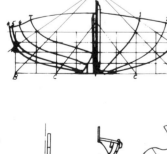

Seaford Skiff by Paul A. Ketchum, Amityville

14' 7" x 4' 3" ca. 1948

Accession No. 1972.264
Catalog No. 7.119

Lines drawn by Robert A. Pittaway, July 1974; sailing rig drawn by Alison H. Pyott, September 1976; construction plan drawn by Chris Rawlings, July 1996

The Ketchum Seaford was the recreational development of the gunning skiffs. Paul Ketchum built about 70 of them for Great South Bay vacationers. He modified the standard Seaford skiff design by using steam-bent oak frames, adding some freeboard, and shifting the mast and centerboard aft—which cut into the cockpit space, making rowing more difficult.

If you're looking for a small sailboat for sheltered waters, you should consider the Seaford skiff. As Barry Thomas wrote in his 1974 article in *The Log of Mystic Seaport*: "If you are ten years old I would commend this boat to you, and so I would if you are forty Nelson Verity when he was over ninety years of age sat at the tiller of his skiff and said: 'I'd ruther be doing this than anything else in the world.' When I am ninety, so would I."

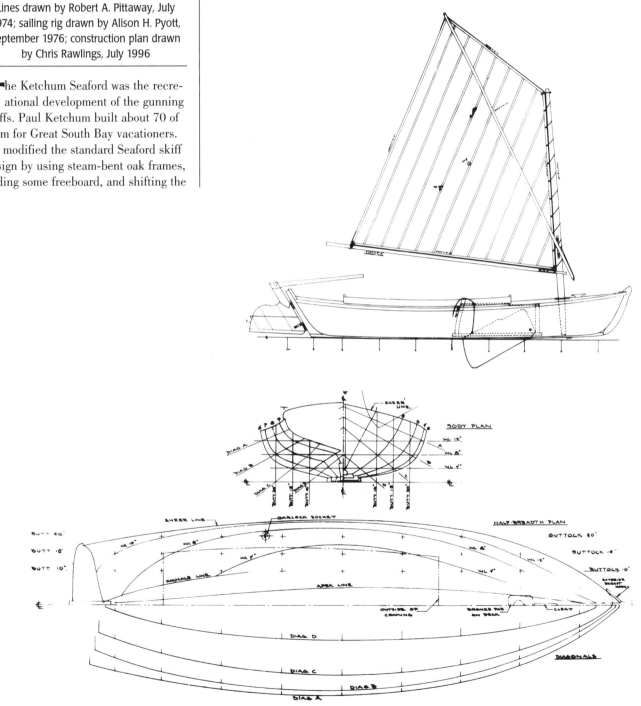

Button Swan
Newport Fish and Lobster Boat

12′ 4″ x 5′ 3″ ca. 1870

Accession No. 1949.145
Catalog No. 7.59

Drawn by Robert H. Baker, June 1975

Small working catboats are rare today; like most workboats they were worked to death. To our eyes, *Button Swan* looks heavy and hard to build, with her 1/2″ lapstrake planks over jogged bent-oak frames and a full ceiling. She features a fish well, essential to the small-boat fishermen who was worked around Brenton Reef, near Newport, Rhode Island. In it, they could keep their catch alive and in good shape for the fancy hotels and cottages of Newport. This boat has no centerboard, relying on a relatively deep V-hull to keep her from making leeway when sailing to windward. Yet, upwind sailing ability was probably not essential, as a Newport fisherman would head out early, before the wind came up. The sail west helped them coming home on the southwest breeze after filling the boat. But if sailing her larger sister, *Peggotty* (Misc.15), at the WoodenBoat School is any indication, *Button Swan* will sail to weather and handle a blow. More importantly, most small cats row badly; *Button Swan* would be better.

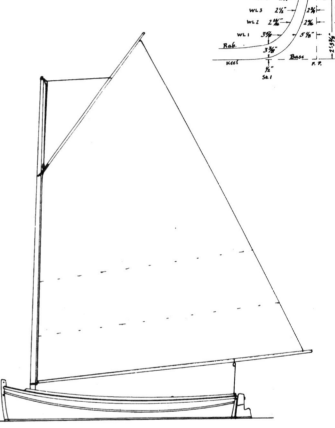

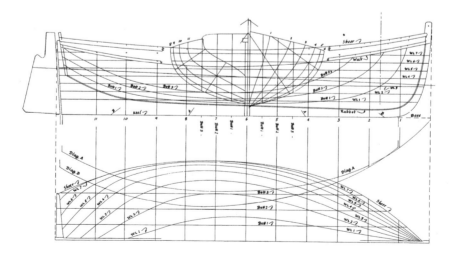

Newport Shore Boat

11' 4" x 4' 8" ca. 1860

Accession No. 1954.1482
Catalog No. 7.15

Drawn by Robert H. Baker, December 1971

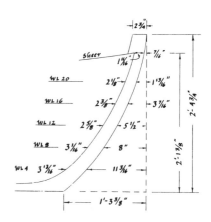

Mystic Seaport also offers plans for *Button Swan*'s smaller cousin, the Newport Shore Boat, a heavily built, 11' lapstrake boat that could be rowed, sailed, or sculled out of the tiny coves that are interspersed between the mansions lining the seaward side of Ocean Avenue in Newport. Like *Button Swan*, she is lapstrake planked over jogged frames and has a well-V'd hull.

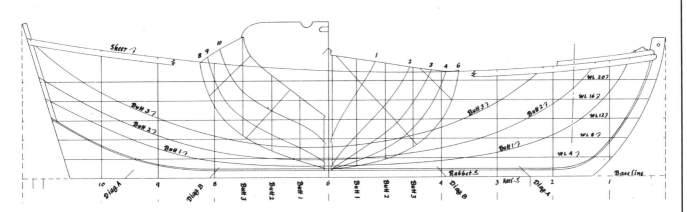

Rhode Island Hook Boat

15' 9" x 5' 6" ca. 1910

Accession No. 1967.201
Catalog No. 7.36

Drawn by Edson I. Schock

Across Narragansett Bay, along the south shore of Rhode Island, fishermen needed boats to get in and out of narrow inlets through the barrier beach, where surf and tidal chop often made boathandling difficult. Rhode Island hook boats evolved there, built like the Newport boats with stout lapstrake planking on jogged frames, and strong ceilings. These were double-enders that handled breakers well. For working through the surf line, they were set up for two to row facing each other. One pulled for power, the other pushed for control.

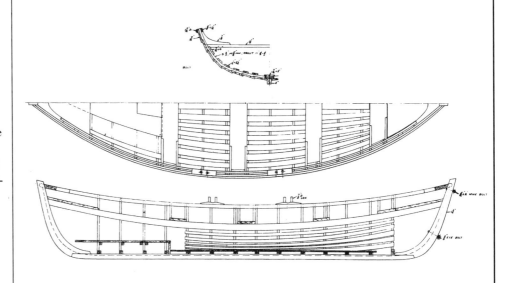

Sanshee
Cape Cod Catboat
by Charles Anderson

14′ 4″ x 6′ 7″   ca. 1900-25

Accession No. 1970.646
Catalog No. 7.50

Drawn by Edson I. Schock

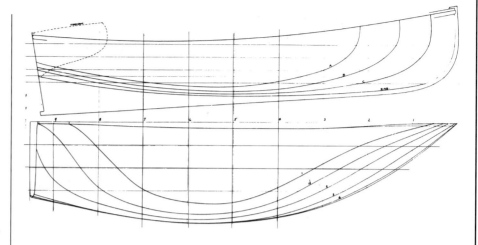

Cape Cod catboats were adapted for recreation after the Civil War to meet the needs of vacationers who began flocking to the Cape. Workboat designs were shrunk to produce boats for day-sailing, and builders began to court the new recreational market. Charles A. Anderson of Wareham, Massachusetts, was one of these builders. A good example of the type, *Sanshee* is about the

ideal size for day-sailing. Her interior benches offer some comfort for a party. She has a touch of hollow in her stern to reduce drag when sailed upright, but she also has hard bilges to add stability

when heeled down. Her bow is quite sharp for the type. She carries 170 square feet of sail to step along well even in a light breeze, and she can be rowed if the wind dies.

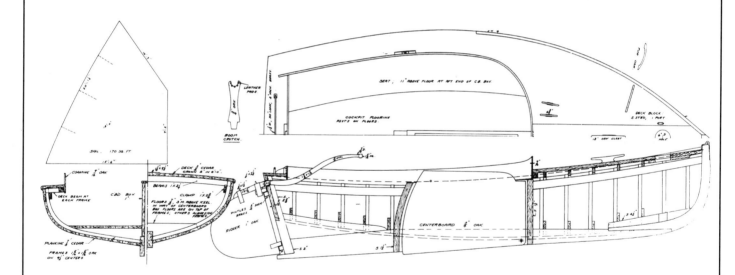

Trio
Cape Cod Catboat
by Wilton Crosby

14' 11" x 6' 6"   ca. 1880-1912

Accession No. 1960.499
Catalog No. 7.53

Measured by Barry Thomas, Bret Laurent,
and Clark Poston, October 1986;
drawn by Clark Poston, February 1987

As a part of the work that would result in the 20' catboat *Breck Marshall*, Barry Thomas and his boat shop assistants, Clark Poston and Bret Laurent, studied and measured Mystic Seaport's day-sailing Crosby cat, *Trio*. In her construction they recognized that the Crosbys had a distinct method of framing their boats. Put in cold, the frames were not beveled, so they rake inward towards the maximum beam of the boat. When they later visited the remaining Crosby yard at Osterville, Massachusetts, they would learn how to do this from Horace Manley "Bunk" Crosby.

Trio is 2" to 5" higher-sided than *Sanshee*, has a higher coaming, and has considerably more bearing in the bow, making her a drier boat in a seaway. Her stern has no hollow, but comes in at a shallow V; all her waterlines are convex. Her spars are longer than *Sanshee*'s, for an area of around 200 square feet, so she should not often need the single sweep that she is set up to carry. Anyone interested in building this boat should follow the method outlined in Barry Thomas's book, *Building the Crosby Catboat*, as the Crosbys worked out highly efficient construction methods.

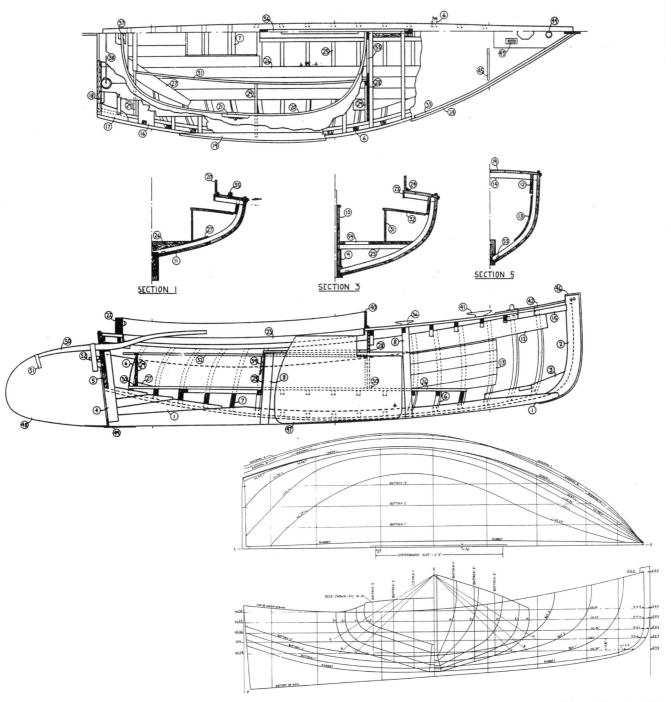

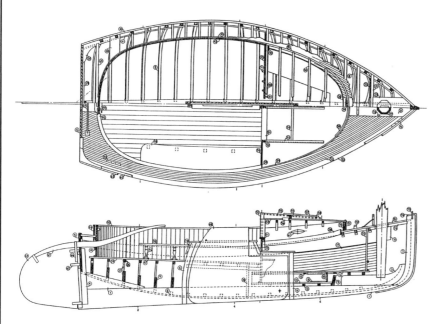

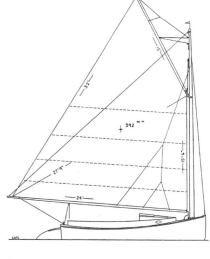

Breck Marshall
Cape Cod Catboat

20′ 0″ x 10′ 0″ 1987

Accession No. 1986.10
Catalog No. 7.125

Based on lines taken from the pre-1900 *Tryphaena* by Barry Thomas, Bret Laurent, and Clark Poston, November 1985; drawn by Clark Poston, March 1987

Thousands of visitors to Mystic Seaport have ridden in the *Breck Marshall* since she was launched in 1987. It is the first time under sail for some. For most of those who have sailed before, it is their first time in a large boat without an engine.

In building her, Barry Thomas and his assistants, Bret Laurent and Clark Poston, looked at all the existing plans and Crosby boats they could find. They wanted one that was modeled without an engine in mind, and they settled on measuring the ca. 1900 working cat *Tryphaena*, which had considerably more V shape to her hull at the stern than did later models. Her stern does not drag the way the later U sterns drag, with the U shape to the hull aft needed to carry the weight of an engine and prevent squatting. Tiller steering, which was common on the older workboats, makes her handle quickly and respon-

sively, which is useful in the close quarters of a Cape Cod harbor or the Mystic River. A sizable working sail area of close to 400 square feet propels her quickly in light air; the first set of reef points is commonly used in the afternoon sea breezes. A gusty northwester means a double reef. Her spar dimensions were taken from a 1905 Crosby sail plan. The reproduction, christened *Breck Marshall* for a builder who did much to resurrect the popularity of catboats, was given the accommodations of a working cat.

The boat shop crew based the construction process on their study of surviving Crosby catboats, but above all they

depended on the help of Horace Manley "Bunk' Crosby Jr., who had worked in his father's shop from 1924 to 1931. Putting it all into practice, Barry found the Crosby methods and materials could not be improved. As he wrote: "This wooden sailboat came at the bitter end of an evolutionary line, the end of a time when men in the boatyard, plus a blacksmith, know how to fashion all of the materials that went into her making. To change this boat's construction . . . would be a presumptive error."

If you choose to build this boat, you'll need Barry Thomas's *Building the Crosby Catboat* as a companion guide.

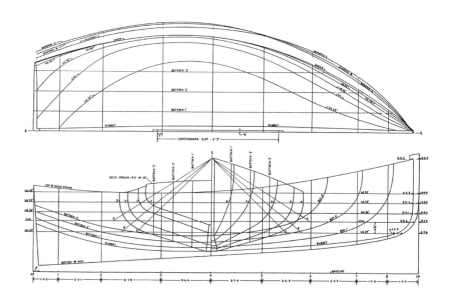

Fishermen at Woods Hole, Massachusetts, on the southwest tail of Cape Cod, had to work some of the worst water in New England. Fierce currents required a boat that could be rowed in a calm, to slip in and out of eddies. Steep, nasty seas created by gusty winds working against that current required a boat rugged enough to punch through the waves, with enough freeboard to keep the water from slopping in. All this was complicated by the need to be able to drop the masts to get under a bridge to reach their moorings in Eel Pond at Woods Hole. The results were some of the biggest 13' boats ever created, boats that were shorter and narrower than a Cape Cod working cat, yet retained the cat's centerboard and high freeboard. When vacationers discovered Woods Hole, they found the fishermen's spritsail boat to be a good boat for recreation. After they set up a yacht club in 1897, the first regatta in 1898 featured spritsail boats.

The three boats built by cabinetmaker E.E. Swift show a highly evolved technique, which is carefully documented in Dave Dillion's plans. The boats also show a steady refinement in design. *Spy* has the least deadrise and is widest down low, while the last boat is sharper all around. The biggest difference is in the position and size of the centerboard. Swift's last boat and *Susie* have the same pivot point, but *Susie*'s board is about 9" longer. *Spy* is in between: her pivot point is 3" aft of the others, but she has the same-size board as the last boat. This changes the interior layouts so that *Susie*'s stern seat is about 10" farther aft than that of Swift's last boat, with *Spy* in between. Swift's last boat is the only boat of the three without batten-seam planking, going up from 7/16" to 9/16" planking to compensate.

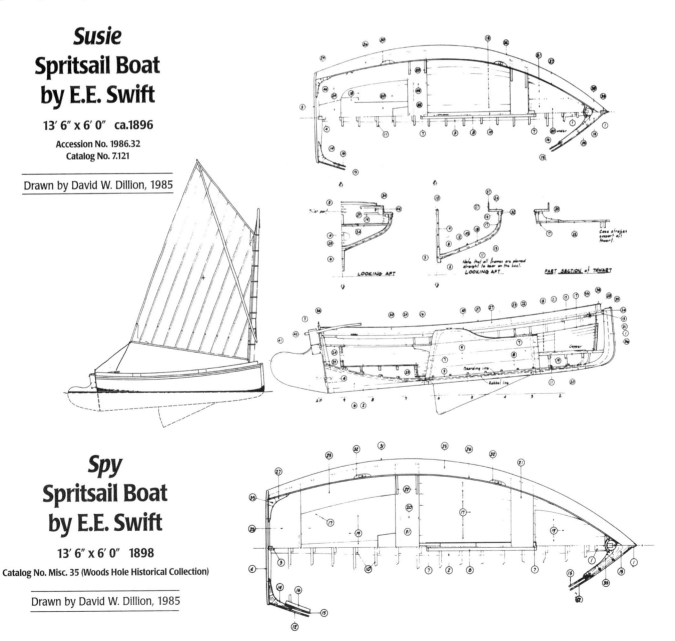

Susie
Spritsail Boat
by E.E. Swift

13' 6" x 6' 0"   ca.1896

Accession No. 1986.32
Catalog No. 7.121

Drawn by David W. Dillion, 1985

LOOKING AFT

LOOKING AFT

PART SECTION of THWART

Spy
Spritsail Boat
by E.E. Swift

13' 6" x 6' 0"   1898

Catalog No. Misc. 35 (Woods Hole Historical Collection)

Drawn by David W. Dillion, 1985

Unfinished
Spritsail Boat
By E.E. Swift

13' 4" x 6' 0"   1913 or 1914

Accession No. 1968.2
Catalog No. 7.122

Drawn by David W. Dillion, 1985

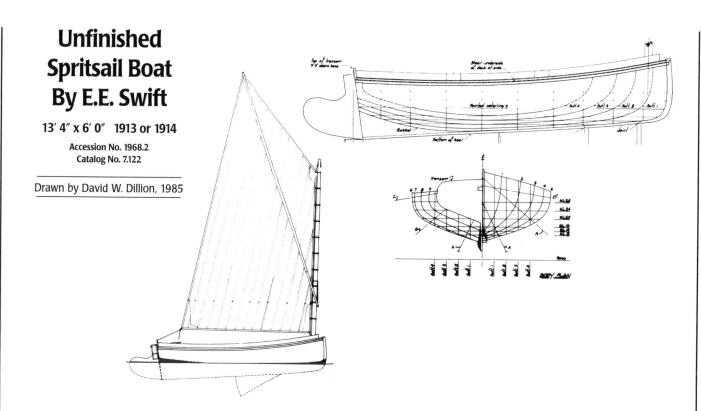

Of the three, *Susie* has the only complete rig. She is the prime example boat used by Dave in his essays in *Boats: A Manual for Their Documentation*, and his drawings give the dimensions of all the sails. For recreation, these boats carried about 90 square feet, for racing about 130. The spritsails are tall, high-aspect types, short enough on the foot so that they can be sheeted to a traveler running on the transom. Since the centerboards change position, a builder might want to check the positions of both sail and centerboard to understand the boat's balance.

Spy won the first race of the Woods Hole Yacht Club in 1898, and won again in 1900, with *Susie* winning a different regatta that year. Swift was building his last boat for his brother, who died while she was being built, which is why the boat was never finished.

Mystic boatbuilders Taylor and Snediker have built a replica of Swift's last boat for John McLaughlin of Mystic. Sharon Brown's account in *Messing About in Boats* 18/7, 15 August 2000, gives you a sense of how this boat—*Roberta*—sails. If you visit Mystic Seaport, you might see her on the river and beg a ride. Or you can go to the Museum's boat livery and take a sail in *Sandy Ford*, the reproduction of Wilton Crosby's *Explorer*, an earlier boat that has a much flatter, more-burdensome hull shape, which was probably more typical of the working spritsail boats of Woods Hole.

Explorer
Spritsail Boat
by Crosby

13' 3" x 5' 11"   ca. 1890

Accession No. 1960.196
Catalog No. 7.54

Drawn by James Kleinschmidt, February 1961; traced by Steen Kokborg, March 1962

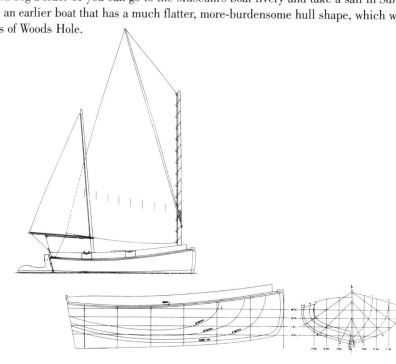

The Delaware River is a far cry from the boisterous waters of Cape Cod. On the Delaware, the artisanal workers of Philadelphia sailed boats called tuckups and hikers. They were all 15' boats, varying in beam and sail power. The smallest were the tuckups, which could be sailed with sizable racing rigs or day-sailed with comfortable spritsail rigs. On the wide reaches of the river below the city, wind and tide could create serious chop, requiring a substantial boat, but the boats also needed to be small enough so that they could be hauled out and stored in boathouses on the busy Philadelphia waterfront.

In shape, these boats superficially resemble Whitehalls, but they are optimized for sailing. A bit beamier for the same-length boat, their hull sections tend to be fuller forward and have a shallow arch midsection like the double-ended Delaware duckers, with relatively less deadrise than you might find in a Whitehall. Freeboard is lower than you'll find in most Whitehalls, with the depth at the lowest points only about 12". Sheer is much stronger, with about a foot between the low point and the top of the stems. There is more rocker in the keel, allowing them to turn faster. Side decks and coamings make up for the loss of freeboard. They have the light construction of a ducker on slightly heavier bent frames.

These two tuckups are built differently. In the *Seeds*, as in a sneakbox, the keel is sprung up in the stern with a skeg added. In contrast, *Spider* has Whitehall-style deadwood with a rabbet line cut into it. The *Seeds* shows how a short stealer plank can be added into lapstrake construction. This was done also in the *Spider* reproductions built at Mystic Seaport to avoid the checking of a wide garboard. We had noticed a split in the garboard of the original boat, which must have happened when she was built. *Spider's* daggerboard trunk is further aft than is the *Seeds's*, and she has a bent cockpit coaming, where the coaming of the *Seeds* is pointed.

The shapes of the boats are pretty similar. *Spider* is an inch or so higher amid ships, and has a touch lower stem. Her transom is far narrower than that of the *Seeds*, and her after sections are slimmer. The *Seeds* has a slightly sharper bow. Both boats are balanced for rowing with a passenger on board.

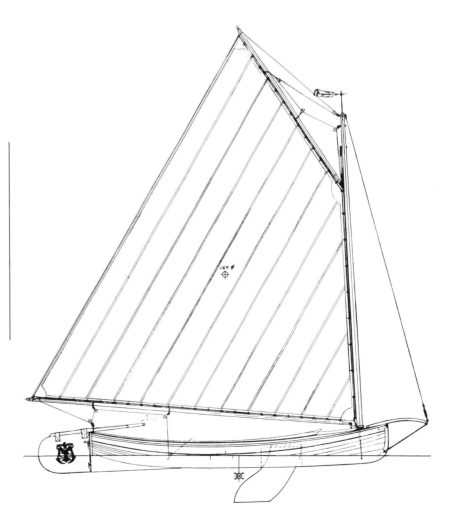

Thomas M. Seeds
Tuckup
by Thomas Ledyard

14' 9" x 4' 6" 1878

Catalog No. Misc. 24 (Mariners' Museum, 1955.1.40)

Measured by Marion V. Brewington
and Edward G. Brownlee, 1943;
drawn by Edward G. Brownlee

To date, I know of seven reproductions of *Spider*. One has a racing rig, and one has a smaller gaff rig like that of the *Seeds* when Brownlee and Brewington measured her. One *Seeds* replica is sailing with a racing rig. Both racing rigs have gone over the side once. For more background and photos of these boats, see "Fishtown Tricks, The Delaware River's 15' Flyers," *WoodenBoat* 148, May/June 1999.

Building either of these tuckups is probably easier than building a similar-size Whitehall, with the added complication of the deck. You'll get a much better sailboat, if sailing is what you want. If you took a bit of hollow out of the transom, you could easily plank a tuckup as a glued-lap boat. Mystic Seaport and some other institutions have patterns for hardware, which is included in the plans of *Spider*. Name your boat carefully, as tradition calls for a fancy monogram on the rudder.

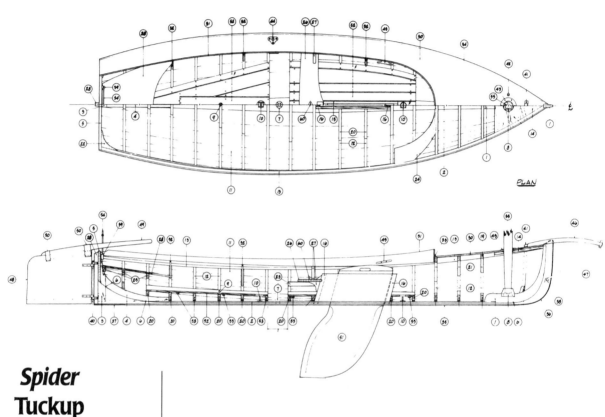

Spider
Tuckup
by Jesse Deputy

14' 10" x 4' 5"   1876

Catalog No. Misc. 25
(Independence Seaport Museum, 1972.21.1)

Drawn by David W. Dillion, 1982-83, after lines, details, and notes taken by Edward G. Brownlee, 1942-43, examination of the boat by the staff of the Mystic Seaport boat shop in 1983 in the process of building four reproductions, and details from the **Thomas M. Seeds** and research into Philadelphia boatbuilding practices

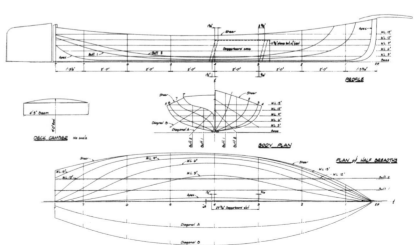

Half Moon
Canoe Yawl

18′ 3″ x 5′ 5″   ca. 1930

Accession No. 1959.1209
Catalog No. 7.72

Drawn by Edson I. Schock

In England, serious cruisers found sailing canoes to be a bit small for the open waters around the British Isles. Several designers created larger versions called canoe yawls. Albert Strange is perhaps the best-known of these designers. Other well-known designers of the 1880s were George F. Holmes and J.A. Akester. A.W. Barlow of Providence, Rhode Island, spotted the design of Akester's 1886 canoe-yawl *Iris* in W.P. Stephens's *Canoe and Boat Building for Amateurs*. He was looking for something a bit different for sailing on Narragansett Bay. He and his son planked her up, added 460 pounds and 4" to her shallow keel, and changed her rig to a gunter lug, hiring a professional to finish the job.

Some years after she came to Mystic Seaport, Roger Taylor saw her in storage and devoted a chapter to her in his book, *Good Boats*, judging her "an admirable daysailer and camping cruiser for protected waters." He felt that she could use a centerboard, as did W.P. Stephens, and suggested reverting to her original full-batten lug rig for ease of reefing. Roger also commented that she'd still need ballast, but movable ballast might be preferred. With a light rig of hollow carbon-fiber spars, I suspect that no outside ballast would be needed, and you might not need anything more than the crew inside.

So why has no one built a replica of this canoe yawl? For starters, her sail plan in the lines is downright ugly, as she was cut down tremendously, or at least her spars were readapted. The sail plan shows a leg-of-mutton mainsail that hurts your eyes. Playing with areas shows that somehow her original boom went missing, as the current boom looks to be about the right length for the gunter. She's double-ended, which means that you might need to row in a calm—not such a bad thing in this slippery shape. Once you got her moving (and if you built her light and left the ballast ashore) she'd move nicely. The ample decking lets her have relatively low freeboard, cutting her windage under oars.

Schock's plans document the way that Barlow planked her: 7/8" carvel with doubled 3/4" x 3/4" frames. Today's builder might want to try cold-molding or strip-planking. Mystic Seaport also has offsets from W.P. Stephens and her original sail plan.

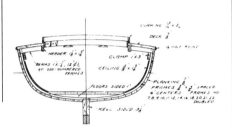

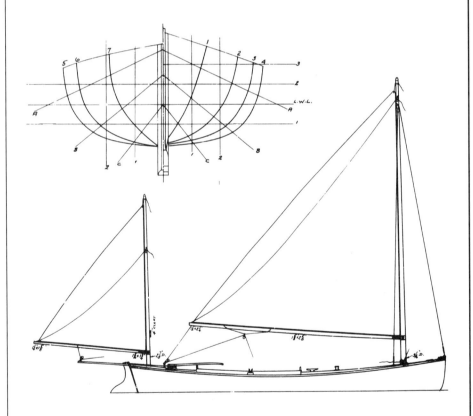

The lobster boats of Kingston, Massachusetts, had to be able to handle changing conditions. Shallow waters and a twisting channel in Plymouth Bay placed a premium on maneuverability. Big tides meant currents up to four knots, a challenge in an under-canvassed sailboat. In a stiff northwester or strong easterly, a steep, hollow sea added to the challenge. As soon as the fishermen were out of the bay, they were confronted with big, powerful, open seas. Today these boats make comfortable, handy daysailers.

Annie A. Fuller
by Arthur Rogers

15' 8" x 5' 5" 1872

Accession No. 1963.818
Catalog No. 7.55

Drawn by Edson I. Schock

Captain Parker Hall, known on the Maine coast for single-handing sizable schooners, got his start with *Annie A. Fuller*, naming her for a lady friend, so the story goes. She was built by Arthur Rogers of Marshfield as a working lobster boat, before racing enlarged the type. Her lines show a nice, sharp bow, as well as a couple of rowing stations, which would not often be needed with her substantial sail area. Double sculling notches in her transom would let you use a big sweep to help her in a drifter.

Spars did not come with *Annie A. Fuller*, but there is an excellent photo from which the sail plan could be scaled, showing Parker Hall at the helm. More data could come from the small Kingston lobster boat in Howard I. Chapelle's *American Small Sailing Craft*. Despite the many years that *Annie A. Fuller* has been at Mystic Seaport, most of them on display, she has been ignored. Possibly it's for lack of publicity. A 1901 article on Kingston lobster boats was reprinted in the first issue of *WoodenBoat* back in 1974. Since then, the type has only appeared in print in *Mystic Seaport Watercraft*.

Too bad. They'd sail rings around lots of fancier, better-publicized boats.

Original construction called for strip planking out of 3/4" stuff. If you did that today, using glue instead of nails, you'd have a distinctive boat that could live on a trailer.

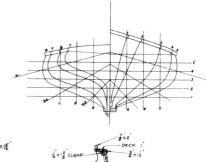

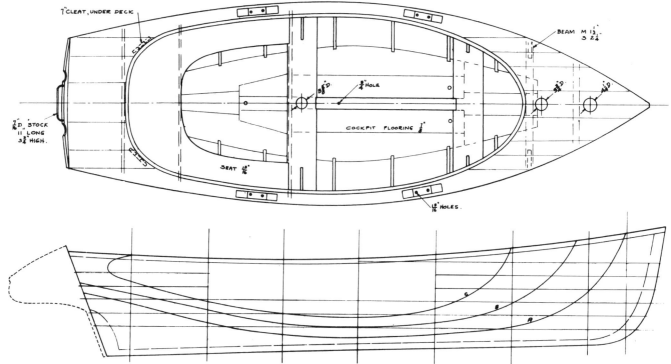

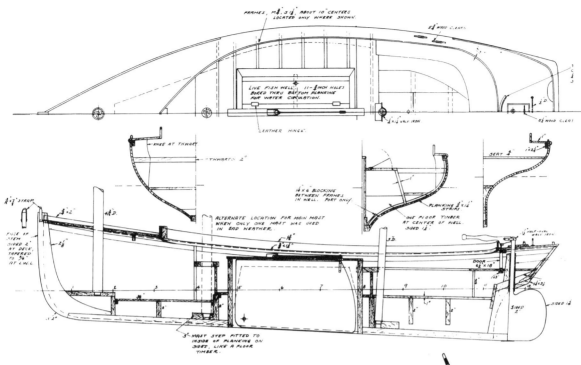

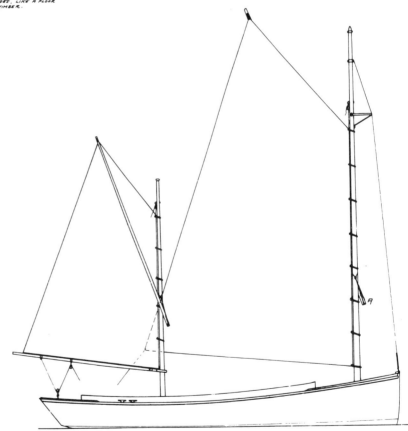

Kingston Lobster Boat by William Bates

19′ 0″ x 6′ 3″ ca. 1890

Accession No. 1956.1544
Catalog No. 7.63

Lines taken off by James Kleinschmidt, February 1968; drawn by James Kleinschmidt, March 1959; rig may be a Kleinschmidt reconstruction

William Bates of Scituate, Massachusetts, built his Kingston lobster boat under the influence of Ransom. Her hollow garboards and short counter stern show the new fashion, but she does not have as much firmness in her quarters, probably limiting her sail carrying power. Like the *Annie A. Fuller*, she is strip-planked. Her third mast step, at the head of the cockpit, makes it easy to sail single-masted.

Solitaire
by Edward A. Ransom

20′ 8″ x 6′ 8″   ca. 1885

Catalog No. Misc. 19

Lines drawn by Valerie Danforth, October 1980; construction and sail plan redrawn by William E. Mills, July 1984, after James Kleinschmidt's drawings of December 1960 and January 1961, and field notes

Solitaire is one of the larger counter-stern and hollow-garboard models, both features introduced by her builder, Edward A. Ransom of Kingston, in this boat. He took these ideas from the America's Cup defenders when he built

Solitaire about 1885. This boat has been owned by two Mystic Seaport staff members. Captain Jim Kleinschmidt, one of the first people at the Museum responsible for the watercraft collection, took her lines when he owned her. Mike Sturges, education and development officer, got her and rebuilt her in 1968. Construction plans were made from the original data verified while taking lines. A memorably unique feature was the massive pair of knees that served both as mizzenmast partners and centerboard trunk (offset on one side of the keel), allowing you to walk end-to-end in the cockpit without clambering over a thwart. She has been rerigged with a gaff main, dropping about 140 square feet from the original mainsail, but making her a little easier to handle than

with the original spritsail. Mike found she went just fine around Mystic in light summer air without the extra area. The Arques School in San Francisco currently has another Ransom Kingston lobster boat under construction.

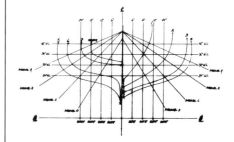

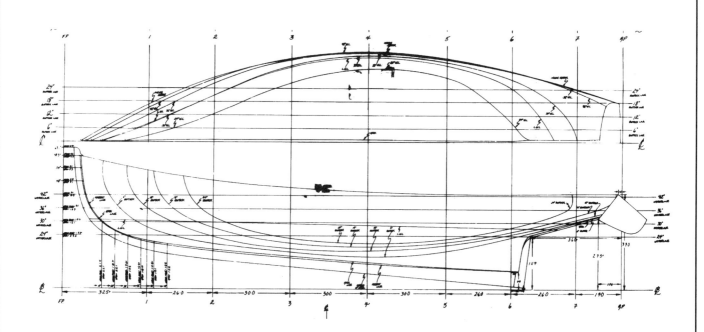

Cuspidor Hampton Boat

17' 4" x 6' 0"   1902

Accession No. 1961.916
Catalog No. 7.61

Drawn by Edson I. Schock; lofted offsets by
Robert A. Pittaway, 1975

In 1902, a New Jersey doctor who summered on Bailey Island, Maine, wanted a boat. He went to Captain Percy Sinnett, a fellow islander, who had introduced square-stern, strip-planked Hampton boats to local fishermen in 1877. For Dr. Luckey, Sinnett built *Cuspidor*, a small Hampton with a powerful rig. She's set up for a couple of rowing stations, but the calm would need to be mighty slick before you'd need to row. Her washboards would help keep water out; lack of a foredeck make it easy to get the 16' mainmast stepped. Put it in the step and walk it up. At 5" diameter, it would be weighty, especially if you rolled the 16' 5" sprit and sail up with it. The mast needs to be stiff, as *Cuspidor* could carry a jib for summer sailing and had no shrouds. Like the power lobster boats that evolved out of these sailing Hamptons, she has a characteristic "double wedge" hull shape with a long, fine bow and a flat run. Her garboards are hollow, and her maximum beam is aft of the boat's center. She would draw about 2' with the board up. There is a bit of flare to the bow to keep things dry.

Like the original, a replica should be built with strip-planking. If she spent lots of time on a trailer, you might consider glueing the strips instead of using nails. And a bit of weight could be taken out of the spars. Be sure and take along a few sandbags that you can haul to up weather to keep her flat in a breeze, as the Casco Bay fishermen did.

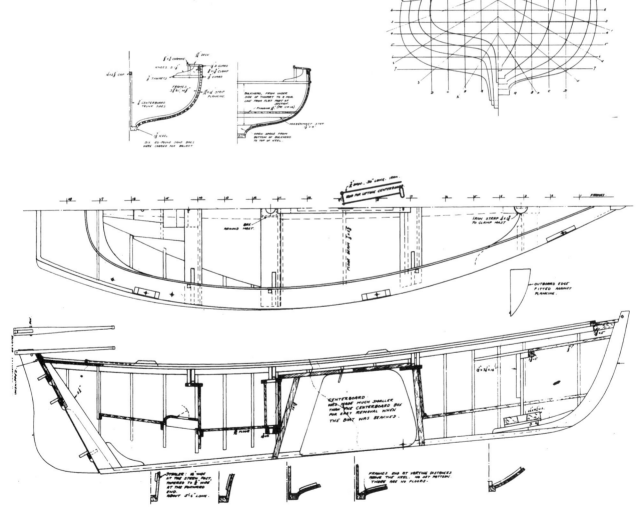

Fishermen and their families living seasonally on Noman's Land, an island off Martha's Vineyard, used small, sharp-stern beach boats for fishing and mainland visits. Common around Vineyard Sound, they were built by boat shops such as Delano's in Fairhaven and Cleveland's in Vineyard Haven, as well as by fishermen themselves. Most boats ran 16' to 18', not too heavy for a crew of two and a team of oxen to haul onto a beach on a wooden "ladder." Centerboards, introduced in the 1870s, were set to drop through the garboard to keep stones from jamming the trunk. Heavy lapstrake construction was preferred for, as Rod Cleveland put it, "Lapstrake would outlast carvel three to one when the boats had to be hauled ashore each night." Extra reinforcements allowed this to be done even when loaded with cod or lobsters.

The boats had fine-lined hulls, with modest deadrise and firm bilges. A bit of hollow in the bow and some flare to the topsides helped keep spray down; like many fishing boats, they were finer aft than forward. Many, especially ones not fished off beaches, had a high coaming set behind narrow side decks to keep sea slop out. The coamings make these boats look fatter than they are. Rigged originally as cat ketches of modest sail area (islanders called the sails fore and main), the boats were re-rigged as cats for easier handling after fishing moved away from Noman's Land in the 1890s. Many of the boats, including these two, later received engines.

Noman's Land Boat by J. Cleveland

19' 9" x 6' 2"   ca. 1882

Accession No. 1952.1115
Catalog No. 7.13

Drawn by Robert H. Baker, March 1972

The Cleveland boat is lapstrake, with a live well for the catch through which a centerboard trunk runs. She is completely open, with short decks only in bow and stern. For strength her frames are jogged over light 3/8" planking. Characteristic of most, her small "mainsail" has a club at the foot to improve sheeting. Bob Baker reconstructed her rig, giving her about 200 square feet.

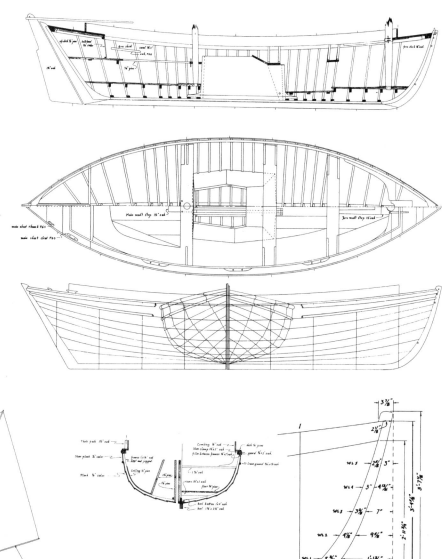

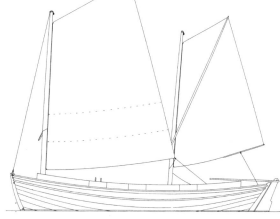

Orca
Noman's Land Boat
by Delano

19′ 9″ x 6′ 5″   ca. 1882

Accession No. 1963.592
Catalog No. 7.12

Drawn by Robert H. Baker, December 1953

Orca is a batten-seam boat that was never used at Noman's Land, rather spending her working life around Gay Head on Martha's Vineyard. She had an engine and cat rig when Bob Baker got her in the 1950s. He rebuilt *Orca* and rerigged her. His plans show offsets and a few scantlings: planking at a light 3/8″ and a 2″ square keel. A prospective builder could more get scantling information from Mystic Seaport. After coming to the Museum, *Orca* was sailed in the summer until the need for major work caused her retirement ashore. Her rig is modest, with only about 120 square feet of sail. Since fishing on a rough November day, with a full northwester punching in, is probably not how you would use this boat today, you might consider adding a rig with a bit more sail area.

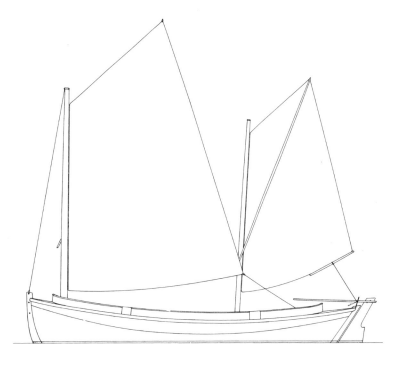

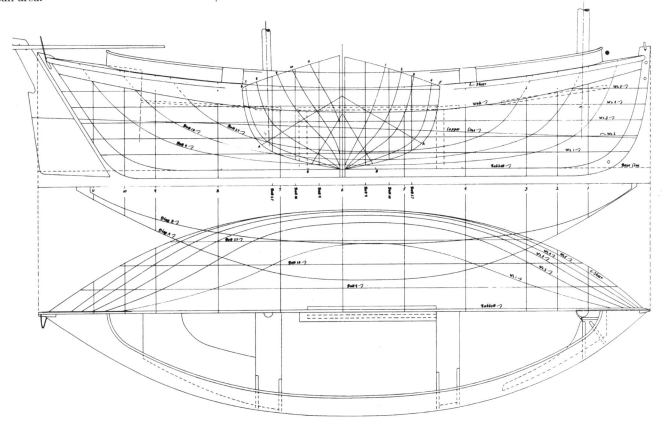

Capt. James Lawrence Power Tender by George Lawley

12′ 5″ x 4′ 5″   1907

Catalog No. Misc. 45

Measured by Robert Allingham and Roger Hughes, December 1995; drawn by Roger Hughes, January 1996

In the days when small make-and-break engines were common and the power to turn large yachts into auxil-iaries was not, yacht builders like George F. Lawley followed the lead of the coasting schooners and built small power tenders to serve larger yachts. This carvel-planked 12′ tender built for the schooner *Blackwing* was loaned to Mystic Seaport for measuring. As might be expected, she is a bit more heavily built than Lawley's rowing tenders and a good bit wider in the transom. When she was measured she had an 8-h.p. Volvo diesel in her, which was probably more powerful than her original engine, but about the same size. Moving at about 4 knots, the engine would be loafing, barely using any fuel. She'd make a head-turning little boat for cruising about a harbor or winding down a river.

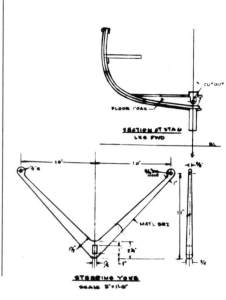

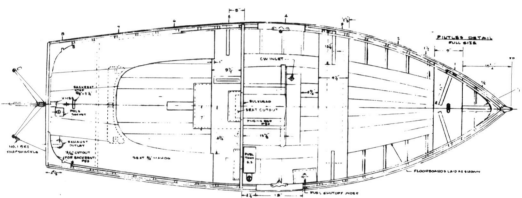

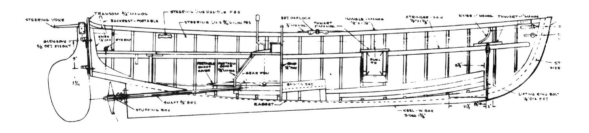

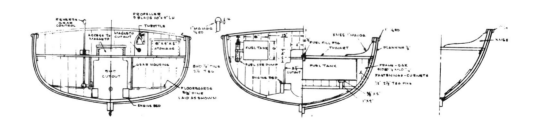

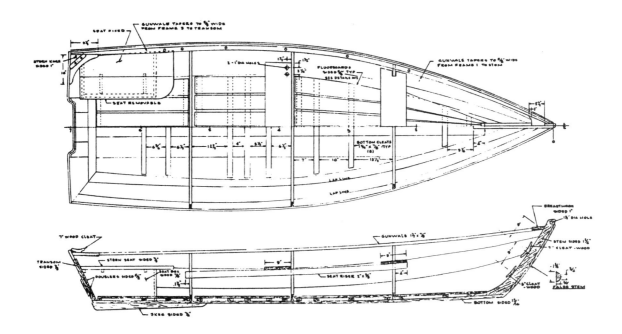

Outboard Dory-Skiff by A.R. True

14' 1" x 4' 8"   ca. 1950

Accession No. 1996.81.1

Measured by Robert Allingham and Roger Hughes, February, May 1996; drawn by Roger Hughes, May 1996

Those in need of a modest outboard skiff might have a look at this one, built by A.R. True of Amesbury, Massachusetts. To take the power of the outboard, he widened the dory-skiff so that her transom is only a few inches narrower than her amidships section, thus giving the boat a bit more eye-pleasing shape than if he'd kept everything parallel. Her bottom, built with fore-and-aft 7/8" planking, has only about an inch of rocker. For trailer work, marine plywood might be a reasonable substitute if you put some runners on her for grounding, or fiberglassed the bottom. Sides are three 5/8" lapstrake planks, and detailed frame layouts give the full plank bevels. The materials are not listed. A unique portable seat allows operators to position themselves for best trim. Anything more than a 10-h.p. motor would be excessive.

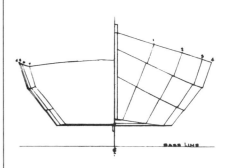

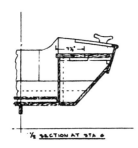

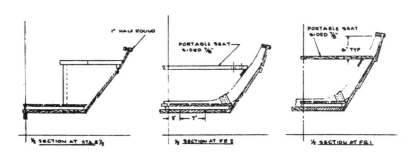

A few of the boats in this catalog have plans for their oars with them. For those that don't, here is a selection. The plans for the 8' and the 7' 9" oars show how they can be glued up of smaller stuff. Both have square or octagonal looms inboard of the locks to help balance them. Length can be changed proportionally, if desired.

There is debate on oar length: almost every boat in this catalog will take at least 8' oars; 7' 6" work better for narrower boats. The spoons here are quite nice; their shape permits you to saw them out of 2" stuff, using a stiff blade in a bandsaw and some blocking to keep things square. For the bigger boats, I find that 10' oars are not too long for a boat with a 5' beam. Be sure and knock off the corner on the handle so you can put your thumb comfortably over the end.

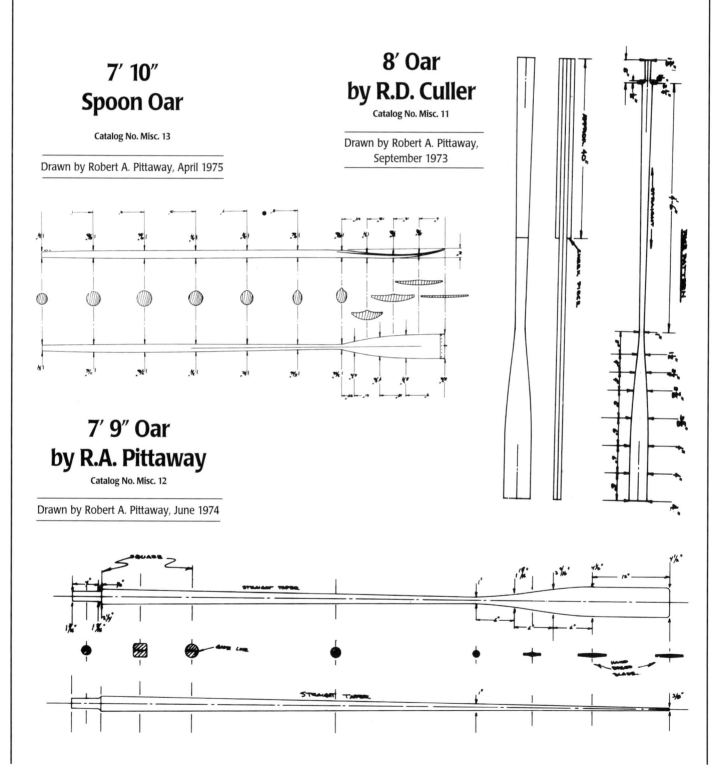

7' 10"
Spoon Oar

Catalog No. Misc. 13

Drawn by Robert A. Pittaway, April 1975

8' Oar
by R.D. Culler

Catalog No. Misc. 11

Drawn by Robert A. Pittaway,
September 1973

7' 9" Oar
by R.A. Pittaway

Catalog No. Misc. 12

Drawn by Robert A. Pittaway, June 1974

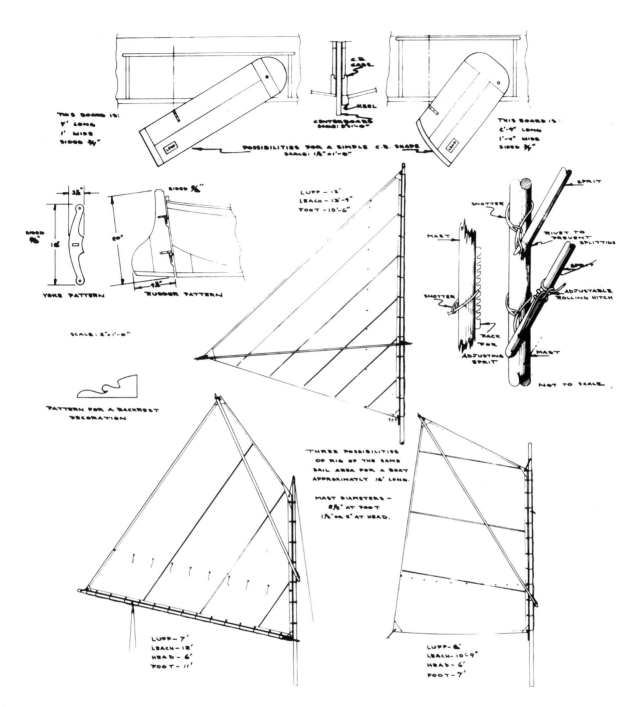

Sails and Rigging Details for Whitehall Boats

Catalog No. Misc. 22

Drawn by Robert A. Pittaway

For those thinking about adding a sail to any small pulling boat, whether a Whitehall, a peapod, or a dory, here are a few ideas. Setting up a centerboard so it drops in alongside the keel can simplify things when you have a scantling keel. Whitehalls track pretty straight, and the rudder shown won't turn you fast. Deeper rudders, common on modern sailing dinghies, however, can be a problem in shallow water unless they are designed to kick up. Old-time sailors often used yokes and steering lines so they could put their weight in the best spot. This is now out of fashion; a tiller and extension can do the same job. The snotter arrangements shown here can be improved. See *WoodenBoat* 165, March/April 2002, for some ideas. Balancing the rig is part of the challenge in adding a rig to a boat without one. John Gardner's essay on the topic in *Classic Small Craft You Can Build* will help immensely. If you do decide to put a rig in an existing boat, make sure that similar boats have them and look at how they are set up.

page92 blank

MYSTIC SEAPORT® Plans List

Ordering Plans

Copies of the plans described in this book, as well as the other plans in the following list, may be purchased from the Ships Plans Division of the G.W. Blunt White Library at Mystic Seaport. Copies of plans are provided for personal use only. Written permission from the Photography & Licensing Department is required for any reproduction, distribution, or publication project.

Plans are reproduced as blueline prints, and microfilm reader-printer copies are available for those images preserved on film. They may be purchased as individual sheets or as sets per boat. Prices for copies vary depending upon a number of factors, including production charges and postage. Members of Mystic Seaport are entitled to a discount. We suggest you inquire for current pricing and postage before placing an order.

Inquiries, orders, and permission requests should be directed to:

Division of Ships Plans
G.W. Blunt White Library
Mystic Seaport
75 Greenmanville Ave.
PO Box 6000
Mystic, CT 06355-0990

For phone inquiries, call 860.572.5360
By email, contact *shipsplans@mysticseaport.org*
Plans information is also available on the Museum's Web site at *www.mysticseaport.org*

The Ships Plans Division is one of the special library collections that are part of the Collections Research Center at the Museum, which is located across Greenmanville Ave. from the Seamen's Inne restaurant. The Ships Plans Division is open weekdays, 9:00 A.M. to 5:00 P.M., but closed weekends and regular Museum holidays. Although appointments are not required, it is best to call ahead prior to visiting in person.

Plans List Details

The following list includes the plans available as of May 2002. The list is updated periodically. The list is arranged by watercraft type. Craft in each section are arranged from smallest to largest. Data denotes the information on the plans: L means lines plan; O means offset table; C means construction plan; and S means sail plan. An R means the boat is recommended for amateur builders. Special features are noted in parentheses.

CLASS	NAME	ORDER#	DATA	#SHEETS

CANOES

CLASS	NAME	ORDER#	DATA	#SHEETS
Rushton "Vaux Junior" Canoe (11')		MISC. 26	LOC	1
Rob Roy (12')		58.1286	LOC	1
Sailing Canoe (14') Wiser		MISC. 20	LC OS	3
Three-Plank (14')		59.1426	LOC	1
J. R. Robertson Canoe (15')		MISC. 39	LO C	2
Sailing Canoe (15')	*Kestrel*	47.1508	S	1
Sailing Canoe (16') (Rushton Vesper model)	*Argonaut*	69.207	S	1
Decked Double-Paddle Canoe (16')	*Chic*	61.262	LOC	1
Rushton Ugo Model Lapstrake Canoe (16')		MISC. 37	LO C	2
Rushton Arkansaw Traveler Model Canoe (17') (Adirondack Museum collection #60.44)		MISC. 32	LO C	2
Canoe, Chesapeake Bay Log (22')	*Fly*	51.4205	LOC	1

DORY/FLAT BOTTOM BOATS

CLASS	NAME	ORDER#	DATA	#SHEETS
Palmer Bros. Flat-Bottom Skiff (10')		96.82	LO C	2
Flatiron Skiff (10')	*Wilbur*	78.121	LC OS R	3
Asa Thomson Skiff (11')		76.148	LOC R	1
Swampscott Dory Work Skiff (12')	*Fat Boat*	MISC. 23	LO C	2
Noank Sharpie-Skiff (12')		MISC. 8	LC R	2
Noank Sharpie-Skiff (12') (Whittaker)		MISC. 42	LOC	1
Noank Sharpie-Skiff (12') (Eldredge)		MISC. 43	LOC	1
Riverfront Recapture Sharpie-Skiff (13') (Add $5.00 ($4.00) for 20 page instruction booklet)		MISC. 38	LOC	3
Chamberlain Dory-Skiff (13')		71.238	LOC S R	2
Amesbury Dory-Skiff (13')		89.94.1	LC R	2
Marblehead Dory-Skiff (14')		MISC. 18	LO CS R	2
Amesbury Dory-Skiff (14')		57.290	LC R	1

CLASS	NAME	ORDER#	DATA	#SHEETS
Decked Dory-Skiff by Chaisson (14')		MISC. 27	LOC R	1
Piscataqua River Wherry (16')		73.236	LO C R	2
New Haven Sharpie (16')	*W.B.*	51.4206	LOCS R	1
Swampscott Dory (17')		74.1025	LC SO R	2
Mass. Humane Society Dory (17')		63.1517	LC	1
Gibben Dupre Creole Skiff (18') (Details)		MISC 41	LO C	3
Banks (18') from Schooner *Black Hawk*		55.320	LC	1
Light Dory (Gunning) (18')		MISC. 3	LOC	1
Banks Dory, Lunenburg (20')		70.686	C	1
McGee Island Chaisson Dory (21')		MISC. 28	LO C R	2
New Haven Sharpie (35')		47.597	LOCS	1

YACHT TENDERS

CLASS	NAME	ORDER#	DATA	#SHEETS
Lawley Tender (9') (Planking information)	*Madelon*	77.254	LO C	3
Herreshoff Dinghy Yacht Tender (11')		74.930	LOCS R	4
Rowboat, Gig from *Dauntless* (16')		38.570	LC	1

WHITEHALLS AND OTHER TRANSOM-STERNED PULLING BOATS

CLASS	NAME	ORDER#	DATA	#SHEETS
Whitehall Sailing type, Cat-Rigged (11')		73.22	LOCS	4
Whitehall-Type Strip-Built (12')	*Favorite*	40.504	LOC	3
Whitehall (13') Livery Model (Van Etten)		73.728	LOC	3
Whitehall (13') Boston		69.584	LOC	3
Whitehall (14') (Partelow) (stem and stern details, planking diagram)		73.39	LOC	5
Wardwell-Built Pulling Boat (14')		49.323	L OC	2
Whitehall, Mystic Seaport-Built (15') (stem and stern details)		74.94	LOC	4
Whitehall (15') (Sheldon)		80.5	LOC	3

CLASS	NAME	ORDER#	DATA	#SHEETS
Lake Boat (15')		73.235	LO C	2
Whitehall (16') (Paddlefast)		MISC. 1	LO	2
Lake George Rowing (16') (Bartlett)	*Winona*	79.70	LO C	2
Whitehall (17') (Bailey)		54.211	LOC	3
Whitehall Model (20') (Sullivan) (construction details)		75.435	LO C	3
Gig, (20') (Lawley)		MISC. 4	LO	2
Pulling Gig from *Noma* (25')		59.967	LC	1

ST. LAWRENCE RIVER SKIFFS

CLASS	NAME	ORDER#	DATA	#SHEETS
Sheldon Skiff (15')		75.177	LO	2
Wilcox Pulling Boat (16')		73.25	LOC	3
Pulling Boat (17')		76.78	LO C	2
St. Lawrence River Skiff (18') (Bain)		MISC. 6	LO C	2
St. Lawrence River Skiff (18') (Hunt)	*Clotilde*	MISC. 14	LO C	2
St. Lawrence River Skiff (18') (Bain)	*Annie*	80.76	LO C	2
St. Lawrence River Skiff (20') (Hunt)	*Bobby*	MISC. 7	LO C	2

HUNTING AND ANGLING BOATS

CLASS	NAME	ORDER#	DATA	#SHEETS
Duck Boat (10')	*Brant*	57.917	LOC R	1
Conn. River Duck Boat (12')		59.208	LC	1
Barnegat Bay Sneakbox (12')		61.915	LOC R	1
Adirondack Guideboat (13') (Blanchard)		MISC. 17	LOC	3
Adirondack Guideboat (16') (Cole) (Adirondack Museum collection #57.192.2) (construction details, oars, oarlocks)		MISC. 30	LO C	4
Adirondack Guideboat (16') (Grant) (Adirondack Museum collection #71.141) (construction plan & profile, details, oars, yoke, oarlocks, etc.)	*The Ghost*	MISC. 31	LO C	4
Adirondack Guideboat (13') (Parsons) (Adirondack Museum collection #64.170) (construction profile, oars, oarlocks)		MISC. 33	LO C	3

CLASS	NAME	ORDER#	DATA	#SHEETS
Seaford Skiff (13')	*Brownie*	62.674	LOC	1
Seaford Skiff (13')	*Ro Ro*	76.149	LO CS	2
Seaford Skiff (14') ((Ketcham)		72.264	LOCS	4
Seaford Skiff (14') (Verity)		MISC. 44	LOC	1
Melonseed (14')		MISC. 5	LO C S	3
Rushton Rowboat (14') (hardware and details)		60.261	LO C	3
Delaware Ducker (15') (rowing)		69.98	LC O	2
Delaware Ducker, York (15') (sailing) (accessories; tent & awning detail)		69.821	LO C S	5
Great Bay Duck Boat (15')		61.559	LOC	1
Rangeley Lake Boat (15') (Barrett)		74.1007	LO C R	2

CATBOATS

CLASS	NAME	ORDER#	DATA	#SHEETS
Newport Fish and Lobster Boat (12') (Swan)	*Button Swan*	49.145	L OS C	3
Cape Cod Catboat (14') (Anderson)	*Sanshee*	70.646	LCS	1
Cape Cod Catboat (15') (Crosby)	*Trio*	60.499	LO C (spar plan)	3
Cat-Rig, Cutter Hull (15') (Harvey)	*Snarlyow*	52.498	LO	1
Catboat (17') (inboard profile and deck plan)	*Edith*	MISC. 10	LOCS	5
Newport Catboat (18')	*Peggotty*	MISC. 15	LOS C	3
Cape Cod Catboat (18')	*Sarah*	MISC. 36	LO	1
Cape Cod Catboat (20') (construction/profile and half/breadth views)	*Breck Marshall*	86.10	LO CCS	6
Cape Cod Catboat (21') (Crosby)	*Frances*	59.1221	LO C S	3
Great South Bay Catboat (21') (Smith)		60.4	LOS C	2
Great South Bay Catboat (21') (Smith) (Mystic Seaport-built reproduction *Anitra* built from these lines) (sections and spar plan)	*Pauline*	MISC. 40	LO CS	5

CLASS	NAME	ORDER#	DATA	#SHEETS

ROUND-BOTTOM WORK BOATS

CLASS	NAME	ORDER#	DATA	#SHEETS
Newport Shore Boat (11')		54.1482	LOC	3
Dion Tender (12')		MISC. 34	LOC	3
Rowboat (12')	*Captain Hook*	74.472	LOC	3
Woods Hole, Spritsail Boat (13') (Crosby)	*Explorer*	60.196	LO CS	3
Woods Hole, Spritsail Boat (13') (Swift) (spars)	*Susie*	86.32	LO CS	3
Woods Hole, Spritsail Boat (13') (Swift) (modified LO / sail & spars)	*Spy*	MISC. 35	LO C	4
Woods Hole, Spritsail Boat (13') (Swift)		68.2	LO C S	3
Peapod, Mystic Seaport-Built (14') (Gardner)		71.237	LO R	1
North Haven Peapod (14') (Whitmore)		85.135	LOC	3
Maine Wherry (14') (Moosabec Reach Boat)	*Temporary*	MISC. 16	LOCS	4
Peapod, Deer Isle, Sailing (15') (Eaton)	*Red Star*	70.638	LC OS	2
Peapod, Cape Split (16')		67.302	LOC	1
Peapod, Maine (16')		59.1472	LOC C	2
Rhode Island Hook Boat (16') (Peckham)		67.201	LC	1
Conn. River Shad Boat (16')		59.808	LO C S	3
Kingston Lobster Boat, Strip-Built (16') (Roger)	*Annie A. Fuller*	63.818	LC	1
Bindal's Boat (Norwegian) (17')		50.1103	LC	2
Hampton Boat, Square Stern (17') (Sinnett)	*Cuspidor*	61.916	LOCS	4
Conn. River Shad Boat (18')	*Dorothy D.*	MISC. 29	LO	1
Hudson River Shad Boat (18')		MISC. 9	LOC	3
Kingston Lobster Boat, Strip-Built (19') (Bates)		56.1544	LCS	3
Kingston Lobster Boat (20') (Ransom) (construction sections)	*Solitaire*	MISC. 19	LCS	4
Seabright Skiff (20')		63.248	LC	1
Noman's Land Boat (20') (Delano)	*Orca*	63.592	L OC S	3
Noman's Land Boat (20') (Cleveland)		52.1115	L SO C	3
Danish Lifeboat (21')		80.149	LO	1

CLASS	NAME	ORDER#	DATA	#SHEETS
Hampton Boat, Double-Ended (23') (Durgin)	*Cadet*	55.318	LC	1
Block Island Cowhorn Reproduction (23')	*Gloria Anna II*	70.763	LS	2
Noank Lobster Sloop (24') (Morgan)	*Breeze*	79.15	LO S	2
Oyster Sloop (32')	*Nellie*	64.1551	LS	1
Friendship Sloop (34') (McLain)	*Estella A.*	57.498	LCS	3
Dragger, Western Rig (40') (Post) (swordfish pulpit; arrangement & details; mast boom & details; outboard profile; rudder details)	*Florence*	82.118	LO C	7
Carryaway Boat (45') (deck & hardware)	*Regina M.*	40.338	LO C S	5
Noank Well Smack (45') (Palmer) (includes deck plan)	*Emma C. Berry*	69.231	LS	3

WHALEBOATS

CLASS	NAME	ORDER#	DATA	#SHEETS
Morgan Whaleboat, Sloop-Rig (28')		68.60	LCS	3
Beetle Whaleboat, Sloop-Rig (28') (Mystic Seaport whaleboat replica #4, 74.1027, built to these lines)		MISC. 21	LO CS	3

KAYAKS & DUGOUTS

CLASS	NAME	ORDER#	DATA	#SHEETS
Eskimo Kayak (15')		65.903	LC	1
Dugout, Oyster (27')		46.643	LOC	1
Dugout, Oyster (31') (includes outboard profile and arrangement)		46.644	LC	1

YACHTS

CLASS	NAME	ORDER#	DATA	#SHEETS
Double-Ended Lapstrake Boat (14')		75.22	LOS	3
Tuckup (15') (Ledyard)	*Thomas A. Seeds*	MISC. 24	LCSS	4
Tuckup (15') (Deputy) (materials, hardware, spars and details)	*Spider*	MISC. 25	LO CS	6
Herreshoff 12-1/2 Class (15')	*Nettle*	63.595	L CS	2
Canoe Yawl (18')	*Half Moon*	59.1209	LCS	3
Cutter (19') (Purdon)	*Galena/Fox*	57.537	LS	2

CLASS	NAME	ORDER#	DATA	#SHEETS
Herreshoff Buzzards Bay 15 (25')	*Fiddler*	59.1286	LC S	2
Herreshoff Hull #718 (26')	*Alerion III*	64.631	LCS	3

POWER

CLASS	NAME	ORDER#	DATA	#SHEETS
Lawley Yacht Tender (12')	*Capt. James Lawrence*	MISC. 45	L CO	2
A. R. True Dory-Skiff (14')		96.81.1	LO 2C	3
Autoboat Launch (15') (Clark)	*Papoose*	63.879	LC	1
Cuban Refugee Boat (20') (V-bottom) (outboard profile)	*Analuisa*	94.130.1	LO C	3
Naphtha Launch (21')	*Lillian Russell*	53.3071	LO C	2
Lozier Launch (22')	*Yankee*	61.1167	LC	1
Yawl Boat from Schooner (25')	*Mertie B. Crowley*	56.1137	LC	2
Racing Launch (31') (Electric Launch Co.)	*Panhard I*	53.3072	LC OC	2
Steam Launch (31') (Atlantic Works)	*Nellie*	56.1085	LOC	3
Steamboat (57') (Adams) (outboard profile)	*Sabino*	73.187	LC	3

SURFBOATS

CLASS	NAME	ORDER#	DATA	#SHEETS
Cuttyhunk Surfboat (25')		41.65	LC	1
Race Point Surfboat (25')		47.1982	LC	1

LARGE VESSELS

CLASS	NAME	ORDER#	DATA	#SHEETS
Ship-Rigged Training Vessel (111')	*Joseph Conrad*	47.1948	LS	1
Whaleship (114') (Hillman) (lines and offsets / construction plan / deck plan and bulwarks / square sails and rigging / outboard profile and rigging / 'tween deck; misc. sections / whaleboat handling and belaying pin arrangement)	*Charles W. Morgan*	41.761		7
Gloucester Fishing Schooner (123') (McManus) (Rigging plan / spar plan / lines plan / deck & bulwark plan / construction)	*L.A. Dunton*	63.1705		5
Three-Masted Schooner (130') (Lines and deck / spars and belaying detail / sail plan, rigging)	*James Miller*	79.76		3
Full-Rigged Ship Model (244') (Lines and deck plan / rigging plan / belaying plan and miscellaneous details)	*Benj. F. Packard*	77.93		3

CLASS	NAME	ORDER#	DATA	#SHEETS
Four-Masted Schooner Model (201')	*Herbert L. Rawding*	81.63		3
(Lines and deck plan / rigging plan / belaying plan and miscellaneous details)				

OARS/SAIL RIGS

Eight ft. R.D. Culler Spruce Oar (drawing and text)		MISC. 11		1
Seven ft. 9 in. Spruce Oar (drawing)		MISC. 12		1
Seven ft. 10 in. Spoon Oar (drawing)		MISC. 13		1
Possible Sail Rigs for Whitehall Boats		MISC. 22		1

RELATED BOATBUILDING BOOKS

BOAT PLANS AT MYSTIC SEAPORT

ANNE AND MAYNARD BRAY

Mystic Seaport's Ships Plans collection includes tens of thousands of drawings representing everything from dinghies to lighthouses. This book describes and illustrates an important part of that collection—boat, yacht, and working-vessels plans from W. Starling Burgess, L. Francis Herreshoff, Winthrop Warner, Frederick Geiger, Louis Kromholz, and Albert Condon, as well as many of Mystic Seaport's own watercraft. There are 128 designs in all, from an 11'6" frostbite dinghy to a 159' coasting schooner, each accompanied by Maynard Bray's astute commentary on the design, the work of the designer, and the context of the boat.

(March 2000) 9" x 12", 207 pages, 463 illustrations.
ISBN 0-913372-86-2 (paper)   1011349 $24.95

BUILDING A GREENLAND KAYAK

MARK STARR

Building a Greenland Kayak takes readers step-by-step through the construction process developed by the author and Mystic Seaport boatbuilders to teach their popular kayak-building classes at the Museum. The design is derived directly from surviving Greenland craft, five of which are featured in the appendix. The construction techniques are adapted for the use of simple hand tools, the wooden frame is lashed together, and the boat is covered with a "skin" of nylon and sealed with urethane. The book is fully illustrated with diagrams and photographs of construction details. Additional chapters describe how to make a Greenland-style paddle and how to outfit the boat, and the appendix lists sources for materials.

(2002) 11"x 8-1/2", xvi plus 120 pages, 130 illustrations, 5-plans, appendix, bibliography.
ISBN 0-913372-96-x (paper)   1020547 $24.95

BUILDING THE CROSBY CATBOAT

BARRY THOMAS

In 1986-87 boatbuilder Barry Thomas and his crew at Mystic Seaport constructed a 20-foot catboat after rediscovering the methods used in the famous Crosby boatshops on Cape Cod, ca. 1880-1935. In this construction guide the author documents the unique Crosby building methods and discusses the importance of preserving and using appropriate technologies from the past.

(1989) 6"x 9", 60 pages, 54 illustrations, 7 foldout plans, appendices.
ISBN 0-913372-48-X (paper)   1011275 $9.95

CLASSIC SMALL CRAFT YOU CAN BUILD

JOHN GARDNER

A renowned historian of boat design and technology, the late John Gardner was at the same time a progressive designer and builder who did not hesitate to recommend modern materials, such as plywood and epoxy, where they can be used to advantage. The 16 designs he selected for this book emphasize skiffs—flat-bottom, transom-stern craft for many purposes—but also include the ancient Gaspé Flat, the Maine Reach Boat, two peapods, three handsome dory varieties, and an early power dory. He also explains how to balance the rig of a small sailboat, considers the suitability of strip planking for the home boatbuilder, and introduces readers to such classic designs as the Amesbury skiff. *Classic Small Craft You Can Build* includes all the design information needed for laying out and building these boats. Each chapter contains a complete set of plans, printed large enough to be read easily. Building procedures are explained step-by-step, making the process easy to follow for novice and expert alike.

(1993) 8-1/2"x 11", 194 pages, 37 illustrations, 66 plans, index.
ISBN 0-913372-66-8 (paper)   1011281 $24.95

BUILDING THE HERRESHOFF DINGHY

THE MANUFACTURER'S METHOD

BARRY THOMAS

The name Herreshoff is synonymous with classic yacht design, including small boats like this one. Here Mystic Seaport's boatbuilder describes how he applied a Herreshoff Manufacturing Company employee's experience to the construction of a replica 11-1/2-foot Herreshoff sailing dinghy. Now in its seventh printing, this very popular book is a "how to" guide and an appreciation of traditional boatbuilding skills.

"For the reader interested in small boats, from any point of view—the historian's or the boat builder's—Barry Thomas has a definite place on the book shelf."—WoodenBoat
(1977) 6"x 9", 50 pages, 47 illustrations, 4 foldout plans.
ISBN 0-913372-33-1 (paper)   1011276 $9.95

THE DORY BOOK

JOHN GARDNER

The dory has seen duty as a fishing boat, lumberman's batteau, lifeboat, recreational rowing boat, and racing sailboat. The most comprehensive book about dories ever published, this is at once a history of the dory, a practical handbook on dory building, and a compendium of 23 dory designs with full construction details. The author, a longtime contributor to *National Fisherman*, and the illustrator, Sam Manning, are perhaps the foremost experts on the subject. A steady stream of letters and photographs to the late John Gardner from successful dory builders worldwide has been testimony to the widespread popularity and influence of this book.

(Mystic Seaport edition, 1987) 8-1/2"x 11", 275 pages, 153 illustrations, 23 plan sets, index.
ISBN 0-913372-44-7 (paper)   1011286 $25.95

MYSTIC SEAPORT BOATSHOP LOFTING MANUAL

BARRY THOMAS

Barry Thomas, Mystic Seaport's boatbuilder, produced this illustrated guide to the mysteries of lofting a boat's lines for use in his boatbuilding classes. It is now available to a larger public in the form of an 8-1/2" x 11" shop manual with plastic comb binding. The step-by-step instructions are accompanied by 25 drawings.

(1998) 8-1/2" x 11", 79 pages, 25 illustrations.
ISBN 0-913372-85-4 (paper)   1011360 $15.95

MYSTIC SEAPORT WATERCRAFT

(THIRD EDITION)

MAYNARD BRAY, BENJAMIN A.G. FULLER, PETER T. VERMILYA

Never before has such a comprehensive compilation of watercraft in a museum collection been published. The Mystic Seaport watercraft collection, largest in the United States, is a treasury of American boat and vessel types. In this new edition, original author Maynard Bray is joined by Mystic Seaport's former curator Benjamin A.G. Fuller and present associate curator for small craft Peter T. Vermilya to describe and annotate the nearly 500 watercraft at the Museum. This includes the vessels accessioned into the collection as well as a number of boats used by special programs at the Museum, and others that are available for use in the Museum's popular Boathouse boat-livery program. *Mystic Seaport Watercraft* features 455 entries covering 140 sailing vessels, from catboat to full-rigged ship; 220 rowing craft, from skiff to rowing shell; 51 powered vessels, from outboard to steamboat; 56 paddling and sailing canoes; and 4 iceboats. The book includes many supplementary reading lists for specific boats and boat types. For easy reference, the vessels are arranged in four categories, according to their means of propulsion. The entire volume is thoroughly indexed. For the historian, the boatbuilder, and for those who appreciate fine craftsmanship, *Mystic Seaport Watercraft* will provide hours of pleasure and will serve as an inspiring reference.

(Third Edition, 2001) 8-1/2"x 11", 420 pages, 721 illustrations, index.
ISBN 0-913372-94-3 (cloth)   1017791 $39.95

FIFTY PLATES REPRINTED FROM CANOE AND BOAT BUILDING

WILLIAM PICARD STEPHENS

Because the plans are missing from most available copies of Stephens's classic *Canoe and Boat Building*, Mystic Seaport has reproduced these plans from original sets of both the 1885 and 1898 editions preserved at the Museum's G. W. Blunt White Library. Descriptive text and tables of offsets are included for some of the plans.

(1987) 17" x 11", 55 pages.
ISBN 0-913372-56-0 (paper)   1011289 $24.00

OARS FOR PLEASURE ROWING

ANDREW B. STEEVER

Adapting and expanding his series in the former *Lines & Offsets*, engineer Andrew Steever analyzes the design and mechanics of oars and their use in fixed-seat rowing boats. His calculations and recommendations will allow recreational rowers to adjust and fine-tune their boats and their oars to get the most out of their pleasure rowing. This technical monograph is offered in on-demand format.

(1992) 8-1/2"x 11", 119 pages, tables, bibliography.
ISBN 0-913372-65-X (paper)   1011313 $15.00

WOODEN BOATS TO BUILD AND USE

JOHN GARDNER

This John Gardner boatbuilding book, a complement to *Classic Small Craft You Can Build*, contains background essays and construction plans for 15 boats that include three dories, the four-oared gigs *American Star* and *General Lafayette*, a yacht tender, and eight powerboats that range from an 18' garvey to a 37' vee-bottom lobsterboat type for commercial or recreational use. As with John Gardner's other books, the plans on the pages may be used to build the boats described. The book also contains discussions of scale half-models, taking off boat lines, specialized techniques in the building of small traditional boats, and the future of wooden boats.

(1996) 8-1/2"x 11", 261 pages, 119 illustrations, 67 plans, index.
ISBN 0-913372-78-1 (paper)   1011377 $29.95

These books may be obtained through your local bookstore, or from the Mystic Seaport Bookstore, at

47 Greenmanville Avenue
Mystic, Connecticut 06355-0990
Phone orders: 1.800.331.2665
Fax orders: 1.860.572.5324
E-mail: *bookstore@mysticseaport.org*